DISCOVERY & EXPLORATION

Exploring Space

RODNEY P. CARLISLE

JOHN S. BOWMAN and MAURICE ISSERMAN
General Editors

Facts On File, Inc.

NOTE ON PHOTOS: Many of the illustrations and photographs used in this book are old, historical images. The quality of the prints is not always up to current standards, as in some cases the originals are from old or poor quality negatives or are damaged. The content of the illustrations, however, made their inclusion important despite problems in reproduction.

Library of Congress Cataloging-in-Publication Data

Carlisle, Rodney P.
    Exploring space / Rodney P. Carlisle.
        p. cm. — (Discovery and exploration)
        Includes bibliographical references and index.
    ISBN 0-8160-5265-4
        1. Astronautics—Juvenile literature. 2. Outer Space—Exploration—Juvenile literature. [1. Astronautics. 2. Outer Space—Exploration.] I. Title. II. Series.
    TL793.C363 2004
    629.4   2003026640

Facts On File books are available at special discounts when purchased in bulk quantities for businesses, associations, institutions, or sales promotions. Please call our Special Sales Department in New York at (212) 967-8800 or (800) 322-8755.

You can find Facts On File on the World Wide Web at
http://www.factsonfile.com

Text design by Erika K. Arroyo
Cover design by Kelly Parr
Maps and diagrams by Sholto Ainslie

Printed in the United States of America

VB FOF 10 9 8 7 6 5 4 3 2 1

This book is printed on acid-free paper.

CONTENTS

AUTHOR'S PREFACE

 When one thinks of the explorers of space, one often considers the astronauts who piloted their craft to the Moon in the 1960s and other astronauts and cosmonauts who followed to staff the space shuttles and space stations. Those men and women were indeed among the great heroes of exploration, to be ranked with Christopher Columbus, Ferdinand Magellan, and such Arctic explorers as Roald Amundsen and Robert Peary. However, the exploration of space did not begin in the 20th century, nor was it always conducted from spaceships.

The ancient human quest to understand the place of the Earth in the universe is reflected in the simple childhood rhyme "Twinkle, twinkle, little star, how I wonder what you are. . . ." The common human curiosity about the night sky, felt by every three-year-old who recites that line, led to great discoveries long before the first liquid fuel rocket lifted off from Earth. In Babylon and Egypt, astrologers sought to link the strange planetary paths through the night sky to human behavior, giving names to the clusters of stars and to the planets Mercury, Venus, Mars, Jupiter, and Saturn. Ancient astronomers such as Eratosthenes and Ptolemy calculated the size and shape of the Earth with some surprising

accuracy by observing the heavens, and they speculated about the physical causes for the paths of stars, planets, and the Moon in the night sky.

From the 17th century, when Galileo Galilei turned his first telescope on the night sky, to the 21st century, when plans to land robotic explorers on Mars were well under way, humankind has sought to use the tools of technology to unravel the mysteries of space. Just as explorers of Earth had used the advances in navigation and sailing ships to reach distant lands, the first explorers of space took advantage of new equipment to study the stars, planets, and moons.

When explorers went out from China, the Arab world, and Europe to visit the peoples of other lands, they were fired by a quest for knowledge, a search for profit, and a natural curiosity about how others lived. When the human race turned its attention to the worlds beyond Earth, similar motives pushed them: a search for knowledge, a desire for profit, and simple curiosity. For all such reasons, the exploration of space is rightly considered as a chapter in the history of explorers and exploration.

Using telescopes, astronomers, as Earthbound explorers, began to realize that the

Earth was only one of several, or possibly thousands or millions of similar planets. Their findings led to speculation about whether other worlds held life. Other beings, perhaps similar to humans, might populate distant worlds, allowing a continuation of the excitement of contact with alien peoples that could produce similar new wealth, knowledge, medicines, and commerce. Space exploration and Earth exploration drew from the same motives and could possibly yield very similar benefits.

Over the centuries, a solid body of information began to accumulate, as the night-sky explorers, some working from their rooftops and backyards and others from well-funded observatories, gathered data. Mechanical precision, glassworking, and lens grinding all advanced, leading to better telescopes that yielded new wonders. By the end of the 19th century, astronomers sought to discover whether there was life on Mars and Venus, the two nearest planets of the solar system. While the surface of Venus remained obscured by clouds, Mars revealed strange markings that appeared to change with the seasons. White caps at its north and south poles suggested a climate similar to that on Earth. Inspired by hints that Mars was marked with canals, astronomers and novelists alike began to imagine the day when Martians would meet humans. French writer Jules Verne and British novelist and historian H. G. Wells founded the literary genre of science fiction, inspiring young and old to build better telescopes and to plan for the day when rockets would lift off from Earth to outer space.

Those dreamers and enthusiasts turned their skills to practical ends, and by the 1930s, fictional depictions of rockets that would go to the Moon and Mars, place satellites in orbit around the Earth, or fire weapons from one continent to another in the wars of the future had inspired engineers to begin to build

them. Through the rest of the 20th century, space exploration was no longer Earth bound and entered a new phase, representing a marriage of science fiction and technological reality. Even as the science reality advanced, science fiction continued to depict new possibilities, with authors such as Americans Ray Bradbury and Robert Heinlein firing the imaginations of later generations with chronicles of life on Mars and with stories of distant empires of many solar systems.

At every stage, however, exploration of space has been fraught with controversy, political battles, budgetary crises, and harsh and hostile criticism that also characterized the work of earlier explorers of the planet Earth. As in all endeavors into the unknown, money and sometimes lives have to be put at risk before there is any assurance of a payoff. It is always impossible to predict whether a voyage beyond what is already known will be safe and make a return on the investment, or will be a foolish expression of human overconfidence, what the ancient Greeks called "hubris."

Even so, for some nations, the risks seemed worth it. The competition between the Soviet Union and the United States for influence around the world during the so-called cold war of 1948 to 1991 drove much of the space exploration of that era. Leaders in both countries believed that the nation with the best technology as demonstrated in the most successful ventures into space would impress others. The U.S.-Soviet competition bore a resemblance to the competition between Spain and Britain and other nations to explore and conquer the New World in the 15th and 16th centuries. As in that earlier era, much was risked, often for great gain, often for disaster.

Out of such competition came the "race to the Moon" in the 1960s, and in the 1970s and 1980s a challenging competition to build successful, permanent space stations. More than once, the Soviet Union demonstrated its ability to make a specific accomplishment first, spurring on the American effort. But as Americans and Russians praised their heroes, they also mourned the martyrs who died in the efforts, sometimes because of the rush to beat the other side to a specific achievement.

In the United States, a newly created federal agency, the National Aeronautics and Space Administration (NASA), was put in charge of these efforts, and that agency constantly pushed schedules of accomplishments and always kept an eye on the reaction of the media, the public, and politicians. There were many historic moments, all well publicized: manned landings on the Moon, robotic spacecraft that toured the planets of the solar system, rocket landings on Venus and Mars, and spectacular new discoveries by telescope.

In the competition for achievements and for accomplishments in putting humans into space, however, the cost both in money and lives was heavy. Critics argued that the risks and the expenses were not worth it. Money spent to lift humans into space could better be spent on Earth, some claimed. Even among scientists who sought more knowledge of outer space, there were many who pointed out that the money dedicated to manned space travel was wasted because much more could be learned with robotic equipment and with improved facilities and laboratories on Earth at far less cost.

All exploration pushes back frontiers, both in the physical sense and on the front edge of knowledge. The heroes of exploration capture human imagination, allowing all people to participate in the adventure of pushing those frontiers. Space exploration, like Earth exploration, holds out promise of such rewards. To understand how the explorers worked and what made their findings possible, one needs to look at their innovations and equipment, at their difficult choices, and at how they adjusted to the risks. One needs to examine the failures as well as the successes and to consider both sides of the many debates that raged around the exploration of space.

1

"HOUSTON, WE'VE HAD A PROBLEM"

 Astronauts Jim Lovell, Fred Haise, and Jack Swigert had finished their first television broadcast from space while moving at more than 2,000 miles per hour in *Apollo 13*, the United States's fifth mission to the Moon, on April 13, 1970. As Swigert, on instructions from ground control in Houston, threw a switch to stir one of the oxygen tanks, a mysterious explosion rocked the spacecraft. Some of the walls buckled with a shudder and a whump. The lights in the craft flickered and went dim, and some instruments went out. Readings from the fuel cells that provided electric power immediately sank to dangerous levels, and the ship spun in a tumbling roll.

Glancing out the window, the astronauts saw a cloud of gas surrounding the ship, together with a clutter of debris.

Lovell, his voice disarmingly calm, radioed command center: "Houston, we've had a problem."

Within minutes, both the team on the ground and the astronauts aboard the craft decided that the only way to keep the three alive was to abandon the main ship that consisted of the linked command module and service module. They would take up residence in the tiny lunar module (LM; also called lunar excursion module, or LEM), that had been named *Aquarius*, after the mythological water carrier.

The astronauts and the three shifts of controllers in Houston, as well as the dozens of other engineers and technicians who provided support to the space program in manufacturing companies and for the National Aeronautics and Space Administration (NASA), immediately understood that the mission to the Moon had to be cancelled. However, the three men aboard *Aquarius* had flown only a small fraction of the 238,000 miles to the Moon and would have to loop around the Moon and use its gravity to slingshot them back to Earth, which would take four days. Whether they would survive depended on how well they and Houston reacted.

LIFE OR DEATH

The LM was designed to sustain two men for two days on the Moon. There was enough food aboard the command module *Odyssey* that could be moved down the tunnel to *Aquarius*. However, more essential requirements were in short supply: water, breathable air, and the crucial supply of electric power to operate the craft. Electricity from batteries controlled the steering and thruster nozzles and kept communications with those on Earth open.

Over the next four days, in a round-the-clock struggle, the astronauts and the flight control team in Houston worked their way through dozens of unprecedented technical difficulties and crises. The breathable air aboard the spacecraft became overloaded with exhaled carbon dioxide. As the level of concentration of carbon dioxide rose, it could impair judgment and create dizziness, and it could finally lead to fatal asphyxiation. To conserve power, electrical systems were shut down, leading to a drop in the temperature inside the craft to near-freezing levels and making it nearly impossible to sleep, and also leading to dangerous levels of condensation of moisture on electrical instrument panels and wiring. Ejection of human waste matter had to be cancelled, with the urine stored aboard in plastic sacks.

To conserve water, rations for each astronaut were cut back, but if water intake went below six ounces a day, it could lead to buildup of toxins in the body. (The normal adult consumption is about 36 ounces a day.) Haise began to suffer symptoms of such poisoning long before the ship approached Earth's atmosphere.

Another concern was the angle of reentry, which had to be carefully adjusted. Too shallow an angle of return would cause the space-craft to bounce off the atmosphere like a stone skipped atop a pond of water. Too steep an angle would burn the ship and its contents to a cinder from the friction of the air. Furthermore, the returning reentry capsule, designed to be carrying moon rocks on its return, would now be too light. The capsule had to be loaded with ballast, consisting of cameras and other heavy equipment that normally would have been abandoned in space had the mission been successful. The trajectory toward Earth had to be corrected with tiny thruster bursts from the LM, never designed to make mid-course changes for the linked three modules.

Sometimes the solution to one problem led to other problems. If carbon dioxide poisoning or toxic levels from limited drinking water disabled the astronauts, they would be unable to execute necessary maneuvers. If power consumption drained the supply too fast, the parachutes might not deploy.

The life or death situation faced by the three astronauts, like the challenges faced by earlier explorers, would require human ingenuity, inventiveness, and courage. However, unlike the historic crises that put at risk the lives of Christopher Columbus, Ferdinand Magellan, and Roald Amundsen, the story of Lovell, Swigert, and Haise was immediately known throughout the world. Television and radio carried the mounting developments to millions of viewers and listeners, in living rooms and cafés, in saloons and in front of television shops. Everywhere, witnesses hung on every word of the astronauts' fight for life. In Times Square, New York City, the ticker of running lights that always carries current news kept crowds informed of the astronauts' plight. In St. Peters' Square in Rome, hundreds of thousands offered prayers for their safe return. In Florida, the families of the astronauts gathered, comforting one another against their personal fears that Lovell, Swigert, and Haise might not return home alive. The world, led by the speculation of newscasters, wondered whether their craft would become a forever-orbiting coffin, a testimony to 20th-century technological arrogance.

FROM MEDIA BLACKOUT TO MEDIA BLITZ

When the flight had first started, the news media had almost ignored it. No major news channel or network had carried the television broadcast from space. Lovell's wife, Marilyn, and their children had gone to NASA offices at Cape Canaveral, Florida, to view the broadcast because it was not aired on local television. *Aquarius* was the fifth mission to the Moon. The American public had become so used to the concept of space travel, that it had become almost routine. Sensing the lack of public interest, television did not interrupt the usual round of soap operas, commercials, stand-up comics, and sports events for something so predictable as another moon shot. However, with the explosion aboard *Apollo 13*, public interest and media attention exploded as well.

For NASA, public attention had always been crucial. Founded by an act of Congress on October 1, 1958, NASA represented an effort to put together in a single civilian agency, programs in aeronautics and in space research. As the agency took on responsibility for manned space travel and as rocket launchings drew close television coverage, NASA sought to construct and maintain a good public image. NASA, as a government agency, of course, had to rely on support from lawmakers in Washington, and ultimately from the U.S. voting public. Good public relations were as essential to the survival of the space program as was good technology. So the lack of attention from the media at the beginning of

the flight was a severe disappointment, not only to the families of the astronauts, but to NASA administrators. However, too much attention on the troubles of *Aquarius* and *Apollo 13* could have disastrous repercussions for the space agency. If the three astronauts died on the mission, the tragedy could create a political and funding crisis that might mean the end of NASA itself.

On a more personal level, the reversal of focus from blackout to full coverage struck Marilyn Lovell as demonstrative of the shallow values of the news media. When a NASA public relations officer told her that television networks wanted to erect an electronic relay tower on her lawn in order to provide constant coverage of her family's reactions, she refused. She asked, If the story of going to the Moon was unimportant to the media, why was the story of *not* going to the Moon so important? If the media did not like her refusal to allow them on her lawn, she told them to take it up with her husband, whom she expected home in a few days.

Another practical problem developed from the public attention. Houston flight command had developed the practice of letting the media listen to the relayed communications from ground control to spacecraft and back. Although much of the discussion was cast in technical language that was almost a secret code, the open mikes, or vox connection, allowed the tone of voice to be conveyed. For this reason, communicators on the ground and the astronauts tried to maintain a perfectly calm demeanor throughout the mission. However, sometimes the astronauts would forget that their every word was being monitored on Earth by millions, and Houston would have to gently remind them to turn off their vox mikes when their tempers flared or they broke into a moment of uncontrolled profanity.

HOUSTON AT WORK

The flight control team in Houston, headed by Gene F. Kranz (who signed on and off as "Flight," for "flight director"), operated from a control room with banks of computer screens. At each screen, specialists monitored different aspects of the mission, each with a cryptic name: GUIDO, or guidance officer; INCO, or instrumentation and communications officer; FIDO, or flight dynamics officer; RETRO, or retrofire officer; EECOM, or electrical and environmental command officer; and TELMU, or telemetry, electrical and extravehicular activity mobility unit officer. In addition, other specialists monitored biomedical conditions, diagnosed mechanical problems, calculated resources consumed, and worked on the spacecraft trajectory. Kranz was supported by advice from the prior flight director, Christopher Kraft, as well as by astronauts serving as capsule communicators, or "Cap-Coms," such as Donald (Deke) Slayton. When Lovell, aboard the spacecraft, grew impatient for the specific instructions on the sequence of guidance commands for reentry, Kraft had Deke, a former astronaut, speak directly with Lovell to reassure him the guidance commands were being prepared.

The astronauts on the ground understood that those aboard the ship might not always trust the ground-based specialists to be fully working in their interests or to share their viewpoint. However, when Deke or another astronaut CapCom spoke directly to Lovell, astronaut to astronaut, it helped relieve tension. Another ground-based astronaut was Ken Mattingly.

Mattingly had originally been scheduled to fly aboard *Apollo 13,* but he had been bumped at the last minute because medical officers discovered that he had never developed immunity to measles. He had been exposed to measles from Charlie Duke, the backup pilot for the LM. Duke had caught measles from one of his children and then had exposed the

other two members of the backup crew and the three members of the first crew of the mission to the disease. All of the five except Mat- tingly had been exposed to measles before. Over Lovell's objections, Mattingly was deleted from the mission, to be replaced by

At the Houston command center, flight director Eugene F. Kranz, with his back to the camera in the foreground, views a broadcast from space as *Apollo 13* lunar module pilot Fred Haise reports in. *(NASA)*

Left to right: Commander James A. Lovell, copilot Thomas K. Mattingly, and lunar module pilot Fred W. Haise pose for a publicity shot before the *Apollo 13* mission. Mattingly was scrubbed from the flight because he had been exposed to measles; he was replaced with James Swigert. *(NASA)*

Swigert. Despite the fact that Swigert maintained a reputation as a swinging bachelor (which did not quite fit in with the image of middle-class respectability NASA hoped its crew would project to the public), he was accepted to replace Mattingly because of his abilities as a first-class pilot.

Disgruntled, Mattingly had to sit out the flight. However, when the crisis developed aboard *Apollo 13,* Mattingly was recalled to work in the flight simulator to test various sequences of shutting down pieces of equipment and developing the procedures for reentry. It turned out that having the originally scheduled *Apollo 13* LM pilot grounded with hundreds of hours of experience in the simulator and a close knowledge of the craft's capabilities was a lucky break after all. The fact that Lovell knew and trusted Mattingly, that Mattingly was a close member of the team, and that he understood the LM so thoroughly meant that his calculations of reentry procedures were accepted as right on the mark.

Perhaps the most striking case of adaptation under pressure was the ground crew's solution to the problem of carbon dioxide poisoning. Both the LM *Aquarius* and the command module *Odyssey* were equipped with CO_2 scrubbers, consisting of canisters filled with lithium hydroxide that would filter the CO_2 out of the air. Monitors used a mercury readout to determine the level of CO_2. The correct reading should be two or three millimeters of mercury, and when the level reached seven millimeters, the astronauts were to change the canisters on their scrubbers. If the level rose above 15, the astronauts would die of carbon dioxide poisoning.

Following instructions from the ground, the *Apollo 13* astronauts jury-rigged a scrubber that used lithium hydroxide to remove carbon dioxide from the atmosphere by using duct tape, cardboard, and a hose from a space suit. It worked. *(NASA)*

Apollo Modules

The Apollo spacecraft was connected to the fourth stage of a multistage rocket fired by a Saturn rocket. The Apollo craft consisted of three connected modules.

As the spacecraft lifted off, at the lead point was the command module with a ceramic heat shield on its nose. Behind that was the connected but inaccessible 20-foot-long service module. Once the rocket stage had lifted the spacecraft into a trajectory toward the Moon, the linked command module and service module separated from the rocket stage. Then, using thrusters, the astronauts turned those two joined modules 180 degrees, linking or docking the heat shield nose with the lunar module (LM) residing inside the rocket stage. Next they backed away the joined service module, command module, and LM from the rocket stage, and the three modules flew as one, leaving the rocket entirely. At the tip of the command module, a hatch connected through a short tunnel to the interior of the LM.

The *Apollo 13* accident occurred in the service module, after the three-module assembly had separated from the fourth-stage rocket booster. The loss of power and oxygen reduced habitability in the command module. The crew shifted from command module to LM to use its independent life-support systems for the return voyage to Earth. Yet, problems arose because the LM was not equipped to support three men, only two in order to land on the Moon before final reentry to the Earth's atmosphere, the *Apollo 13* crew moved back into the command module, then separated from the LM, and finally from the damaged service module. The heat shield–protected command module plummeted back through the Earth's atmosphere, slowing from air friction to a speed at which parachutes could permit a soft landing in the ocean, near waiting U.S. Navy ships.

However, the small scrubber in the LM was insufficient in capacity to remove the gas from the air. The larger canister in the command module scrubber could do the job, but it had to be connected to the air system in the LM. Designers had made the two scrubbers completely differently, with the command module scrubber canister in a large square box, and the connections in the LM scrubber designed for a smaller, circular fitting.

A ground team headed by Ed Smylie came up with a solution. Working with the same equipment found aboard the spacecraft— including cooling tubing from underwear to be worn under the space suits while walking on the Moon, duct tape, and a flexible cover taken off a loose-leaf binder flight plan— Smylie's designers put together an invention that adapted the command module scrubber filter to the smaller LM connections. As Lovell and Swigert tried to nap, the readings on the CO_2 monitor climbed to 13, dangerously close to the poisoning mark. Lovell and Swigert joined Haise in gathering the materials needed to replicate Smylie's contraption: scissors, duct tape, flight-book covers, command module canisters, and tubing. Then, in a detailed reading of step-by-step assembly instructions, the team aboard *Aquarius* put together the same device designed by Smylie's group, piecing together the parts, each described carefully and oriented up and down, left and right by remote, relayed instructions.

The astronauts turned on the scrubber, and after a few anxious moments, the odd little duct-taped gadget began to work. The mercury level on the CO_2 monitor fell to 12, then down to 10 and below.

SPLASHDOWN

One by one, the technical problems were solved on the ground and in space by the astronauts. With Haise suffering from a fever, and all three astronauts exhausted from interrupted sleep and freezing temperatures, the

When the *Apollo 13* crew separated their command module from the damaged service module, it slowly turned away, and they caught this picture of the damage. An entire panel had blown out in an apparent explosion of an oxygen tank. *(NASA)*

Distance and Time

For the crew, *Apollo 13*'s planned loop around the Moon and back to Earth would be a very long and risky trip in the annals of exploration. The distance from the Earth to the Moon is about 240,000 miles, but the precise distance varies because the path of the Moon around Earth is an ellipse, rather than a circle. At its closest approach to Earth, the Moon is 221,463 miles away. The mean distance is 238,857 miles. Even these figures are bit on the high side because they represent the distance measured from the center of the Earth to the center of the Moon. Since the Earth has a diameter of 7,926 miles at the equator, and the Moon has a diameter of 2,160 miles, the distance between the surface of Earth and the surface of the Moon is about 5,043 miles less than the distance between the centers. So at the closest approach of Earth and Moon, the one-way direct distance is about 216,420 miles. The Apollo spacecraft, however, made orbits around the Moon, rather than direct surface-to-surface flights. When Christopher Columbus sailed to the Bahamas, Cuba, and Hispaniola and back to Spain in 1492, the distance traveled was less than 10,000 miles. When Sebastian del Cano (who took over the *Victoria* after the death of Ferdinand Magellan) completed the circumnavigation of the Earth in 1522, he and the surviving crew traveled 42,000 miles, counting their long routes around South America and Africa. It had taken del Cano and crew nearly three years. In 1970, for the *Apollo 13* crew, if all went well after the accident, the nearly half-million-mile round trip would take four days.

men transferred back into the command module to use it as a descent capsule. Separating the modules, the three said good-bye to the LEM that had been their home for more than three trying days. Then, as they separated the command module with its heat shield from the main body of the 20-foot-long service module that held oxygen tanks, fuel cells, and propulsion motors, the damaged service module slowly turned away

The *Apollo 13* crew had already been rescued from the sea when the crew aboard the U.S. Navy ship *Iwo Jima* hoisted aboard the *Odyssey* capsule that had been their lifeboat in space. *(NASA)*

Left to right: Fred Haise, Jim Lovell, and Jack Swigert step down from the rescue helicopter aboard the *Iwo Jima.* (NASA)

into space. Only then could the crew view through their windows the blown-out side of the service module. Although the original explosion had seemed for a moment like a meteor collision, it became clear that an oxygen tank had blown up, probably caused by a defective electrical connection in the machine in the tank that was to stir the oxygen. The astronauts hurriedly snapped a few photographs of the damaged service module before returning to their stations for reentry.

Slanting into the atmosphere at some 25,000 miles per hour, the heat shield on the base of the *Odyssey* module heated up to 5,000 degrees Fahrenheit or more, breaking the air into a radiation shower of ions (charged subatomic particles) as it streaked toward its splashdown site in the Pacific Ocean. Below on Earth, listeners waited through a minute of radio silence, as communications were broken by the heat shield's ion burst. If the shield broke, the ship would disintegrate and the astronauts would be incinerated. Nervously,

Astronaut James A. Lovell, commander of the *Apollo 13*, relates to the members of the Senate Space Committee in an open session the problems of the mission. *(NASA)*

CapCom Joe Kerwin radioed: "*Odyssey,* Houston standing by, over."

The seconds ticked by with no response. The message repeated: "*Odyssey,* Houston standing by, over." No response.

Then the static level changed, and Swigert's voice came on, responding, "OK, Joe." The assembled team broke into applause, and around the world, as the words were relayed, millions of others listening to the radio and watching the television heaved a sigh of relief. Minutes later, the spacecraft's first small drogue parachutes opened. The drogues were designed to pull out larger ones that, in turn, eventually pulled out the three main parachutes that floated the capsule at a gentle 20 miles per hour down to the ocean, a few hundred yards from waiting U.S. Navy ships. A helicopter was deployed to lift them from the sea.

The astronauts were safe. Space travel had demonstrated that exploration continued to require brave individuals who would risk their lives, just as explorers on land and sea had done before them.

2

EXPLORING THE UNIVERSE
From Ptolemy to Newton and Beyond

 Long before the first rockets lifted Soviet cosmonauts and American astronauts into space, humans explored the universe without leaving the surface of Earth. In the centuries before electric light, the starry skies, even over the biggest cities, were a spectacular display of pinpoints of light. The puzzles presented by the stars fascinated wise men, priests, and ordinary people. For observers in the Northern Hemisphere, from Babylon to Egypt, from Athens to Rome, and in the Mayan observatories of Mesoamerica, the stars seemed to rotate slowly in the heavens around an imaginary point that was due north.

EXPLORING THE NIGHT SKY BEFORE TELESCOPES

There were perplexing aspects to the way the night sky looked. People wondered: What were the stars, and how far away were they? Why did some steady spots of light appear to wander out of order with the other glittering stars in irregular paths from night to night? Did the patterns or constellations of the stars have any special, mysterious meaning? The Sun rose in the morning at different times of the year against the point on the horizon where different constellations had faded out with the dawn's light. Babylonian observers called the string of constellations the Zodiac, and they gave the twelve constellations names, in groups of three, depending on the season. The dots of light in each constellation, when connected with imaginary lines, presented the outlines of mythical beings. They ranged from Aries (the Ram) and Taurus (the Bull) to Aquarius (the Waterbearer), and Pisces (the Fishes).

Using these peculiar patterns, the ancient Babylonians invented the magical concept of astrology, making calculations from a person's date of birth to cast predictions about the influence of the stars on the individual's life. Although today astrology lives on, modern science rejects its logic. But on a clear night, modern sky watchers can still discern the slow passage of the same constellations identified thousands of years ago.

The ancient astrologers collected details, named the constellations and many of the brightest stars, and identified the motions of the wandering planets that they could see: Mercury, Venus, Mars, Jupiter, and Saturn. The exploration of the universe had begun, but its meaning and the way it worked remained full of mystery.

Space explorers who sought a rational, rather than mystical explanation before the invention of the telescope used the tools of logic, mathematics, and physics to put together answers. One theory, developed by a Greek astronomer living in Egypt, Ptolemy (A.D. 100–170), took into account the motions of the planets and the stars. Ptolemy reasoned that something in the sky had to be holding up the brilliant points of light that were stars. In his work the *Almagest,* he proposed that a series of invisible crystalline spheres, one nested inside the other, carried the stars and planets. The spheres rotated about the Earth,

Native American Astronomy

In the ancient cultures of the Western Hemisphere, including those of the Plains Indians, Aztec, Maya, and Inca, astronomical observation reached an advanced state. Mayan astronomer-priests in southern North America carefully recorded the motions of the Sun, the planet Venus, and the constellation Sirius. At Uxmal, a Mayan site in the Yucatán Peninsula in Mexico, archaeologists have discovered that the city's buildings were precisely aligned with planets and stars.

The Maya and Aztec used a double calendar: One was based on the precisely recorded cycles of Venus, producing a year that was 260 days long; the other was based on the motions of the Sun, establishing a year that was 365 days long. The dates in the two calendars would repeat every 52 years in groups of years called "year bundles" that were used to record historical events. At one site outside the city of Oaxaca in Mexico, a stone carved about 2,500 years ago displayed elements of the 260-day calendar.

In what is now the state of New Mexico, the ancient Anasazi built structures in Chaco Canyon that have windows and niches that precisely line up the Sun's beams on the longest day of the year, the summer solstice. Stone monuments known as "medicine wheels," built some 2,600 years ago in Montana and the Canadian province of Saskatchewan, also line up with the Sun at summer solstice and with the constellation Sirius on the night of the solstice.

Archaeologists have speculated about the role such monuments, calendars, and structures played in the general culture. In some areas, it was clear that the close observation of the stars had practical purposes such as identifying the best times for planting crops and for keeping track of the passage of the years. But in other areas, the alignments and records seemed to have had religious and more ceremonial significance.

In this fanciful portrait, Aristotle, who lived in the third century B.C., meets with Ptolemy, from the second century A.D., and Nicolaus Copernicus, from the 16th century A.D., to discuss their views of astronomy. *(Library of Congress, Prints and Photographs Division [LC-USZ62-95172])*

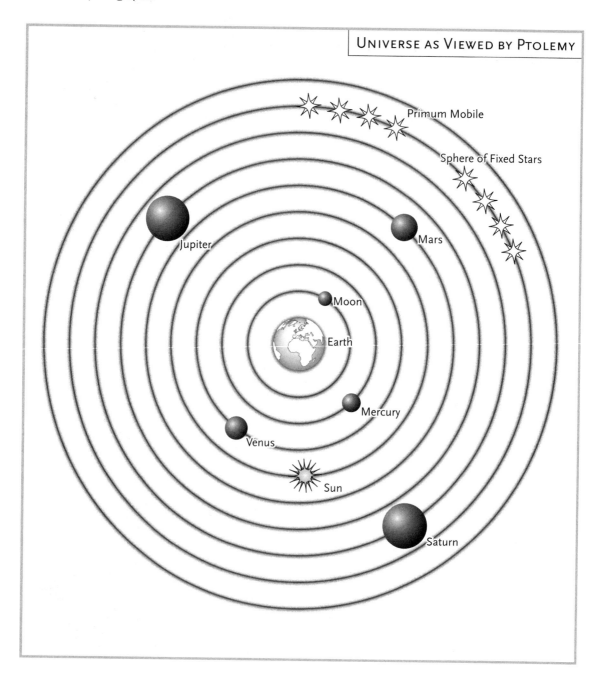

UNIVERSE AS VIEWED BY PTOLEMY

Primum Mobile

Sphere of Fixed Stars

Jupiter

Mars

Moon

Earth

Mercury

Venus

Sun

Saturn

he explained. The planets, as well as the Sun and Moon, each on a different sphere, passed around the Earth, which was at the center of the universe, standing still.

There were several attractive aspects about this explanation. For one thing, it seemed to follow common sense: It certainly appeared that the Earth stood still and that the Sun,

Moon, and stars moved across the sky. The invisible crystalline spheres holding up the stars also seemed to be sensible, because items in the sky would fall if not held up. For another thing, it seemed that the stars and planets did move around the Earth, but in different pathways. Ptolemy's crystalline spheres were an imaginary exploration of space, and his theory was convincing, as it was based on visible, tangible evidence. European scientists and scholars accepted Ptolemy's explanation for more than 1,500 years, adding refinements to his ideas to explain new details and contradictory aspects. One curiosity, for example, was that the planets appeared to stop and reverse course before moving forward again. Separate, contrarotating spheres had to be added to explain the retrograde motion—a complicated, but still workable solution.

FIRST EXPLORATION WITH THE TELESCOPE

Sometime between A.D. 1280 and 1286, an inventor developed eyeglasses, probably in or near Venice, Italy. Within 20 years, people across Europe were wearing spectacles to improve their eyesight. About 300 years later, an eyeglass lens maker, Hans Lippershey of Holland, discovered that he could mount two lenses in a line and achieve magnification of distant objects. Lippershey made the first telescope in 1608. Word of his idea spread rapidly from country to country.

In Italy, Galileo Galilei (1564–1642), a math professor and physics experimenter at the University of Padua, heard of the Lippershey device and built one for himself. Galileo (he was known to history by his first name) was the first explorer of the universe to use the telescope, turning it first on the Moon, then on the planets. He found a number of new and exciting facts. Although astronomers had assumed all objects in the heavens to be made

of "heavenly," or perfect, material, he found that the Moon was covered with mountains and craters and what appeared to be dark seas. Furthermore, he found that Venus, assumed to be a perfect disk of light, was in fact like the Moon in that it had phases. Jupiter, he discovered, was surrounded by four small moons that rotated around it. The Sun itself had sunspots that moved across the face of the Sun, either from the Sun's own movement or the movement of Earth. Galileo quickly reported his discoveries in a short publication, *Siderius Nuncius* (Starry messenger), in March 1610.

The discoveries of Galileo came at just the right time to make for a revolution in the thinking about the universe. More than sixty years before, in 1543, Nicolaus Copernicus

Galileo Galilei built a telescope, and his first observations of the planets tended to confirm the ideas of Nicolaus Copernicus published more than a half-century earlier. *(Library of Congress, Prints and Photographs Division [LC-USZ62-103175])*

(1473–1543), a Polish churchman and scientist, had suggested that Ptolemy's view of the universe with the Earth at the center and the stars rotating around it might be wrong. In *De revolutionibus orbium coelestium* (On the revolutions of the celestial spheres), he proposed a different theory, with the Sun at the center and Earth and the other planets rotating around the Sun. His alternative explanation, known as a heliocentric (Sun-centered) system as opposed to Ptolemy's geocentric (Earth-centered) system, was under debate when Galileo published *Siderius Nuncius*. Some thought the heliocentric idea made better sense and explained the odd motions of the planets better. Others thought it flew in the face of accepted astronomy and that it even contradicted statements in the Bible.

When Galileo's *Siderius Nuncius* came out offering new discoveries that he had found through exploring the universe with his new telescope, it fitted right into the debate over the ideas of Copernicus. Several facts made Galileo's study even more controversial. For one thing, the 1543 edition of Copernicus's *De revolutionibus* included a disclaimer suggesting that the heliocentric view was simply an alternative explanation, not an assertion that Copernicus was right or that Ptolemy was wrong. However, in 1610, Galileo was now offering some facts that backed up heliocentrism as not just an alternative but a *better* explanation. Perhaps the most striking aspect of his discoveries was that Jupiter, like Earth, had its own moons. Furthermore, the mountains on the Moon suggested that heaven and Earth were more similar than anyone had supposed. Much of the exploration and discovery from the telescope seemed to support the new and controversial ideas of Copernicus.

Other aspects of the writing and research turned Galileo's ideas into instant contro-

Nicolaus Copernicus proposed a model of the universe with the Sun at the center and the planets revolving around it. His ideas were published in the year of his death and proved revolutionary in more ways than one. *(Library of Congress, Prints and Photographs Division [LC-USZ62-96983])*

versies. Galileo loved to argue, and he was a master of "disputation," a method of teaching that pitted one view against another. He not only adopted the method as style, he was good at it and appeared to revel at putting down his opponents. As a consequence, he left a trail of hurt feelings and disgruntled and defeated disputants, including some who looked for a chance to discredit him. Another reason that Galileo's findings ran into criticism derived from the fact that since the time of Copernicus, the Roman Catholic Church had become increasingly

net, in quo terram cum orbe lunari tanquam epicyclo contineri diximus. Quinto loco Venus nono menſe reducitur. Sextum deniq; locum Mercurius tenet, octuaginta dierum ſpacio circũ currens. In medio uero omnium reſidet Sol. Quis enim in hoc

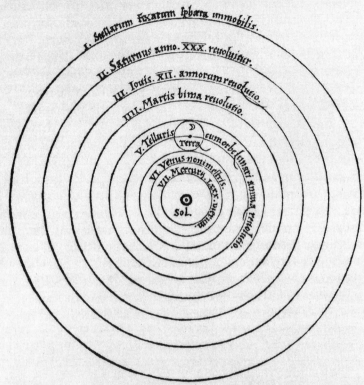

pulcherimo templo lampadem hanc in alio uel meliori loco po neret, quàm unde totum ſimul poſsit illuminare? Siquidem non inepte quidam lucernam mundi, alij mentem, alij rectorem uo= cant. Trimegiſtus uiſibilem Deum, Sophoclis Electra intuentẽ omnia. Ita profecto tanquam in ſolio re gali Sol reſidens circum agentem gubernat Aſtrorum familiam. Tellus quoq; minime fraudatur lunari miniſterio, ſed ut Ariſtoteles de animalibus ait, maximã Luna cũ terra cognatio nẽ habet. Concipit interea à Sole terra, & impregnatur annuo partu. Inuenimus igitur ſub hac

In *De revolutionibus*, 1543, Copernicus included this diagram of the orbits of the planets. *(Library of Congress, Prints and Photographs Division [LC-USZ62-95165])*

The Telescope and the Inquisition

In 1517, Martin Luther, a German Catholic priest, publicly tacked up a list of 95 criticisms of church practices, including taking cash donations in exchange for forgiveness of sins. Luther intended his protest to lead to reforms within the church; instead, he was excommunicated from the church, and his followers were dubbed Protestants and set up independent churches. The movement became known as the Reformation. In much of Europe, the Catholic Church, based in Rome and headed by the pope, continued to exert its authority through the appointment of clergymen and through influence on civil governments. Independent Protestant churches, however, spread increasingly through northern and central Europe.

The Catholic Church responded to the Reformation in diverse ways, trying to control the spread of independent ideas. On the one hand, it instituted the Counter-Reformation, a series of internal reforms. On the other hand, the church set up several "thought-control" methods, such as preapproving books for publication by requiring an imprimatur, or stamp of approval, from a church official. Rejected books were placed on the *Index of Prohibited Books.* Investigation boards, known as inquisitions—after the Congregation of the Inquisition, an institution based in Rome—held hearings to determine whether an individual had violated religious principles. Sometimes, under the Inquisition suspects were tortured to obtain confessions. If the Inquisition found persons guilty of heresy, they would be turned over to the civil authority for punishment, which sometimes included execution.

Galileo Galilei's personal enemies denounced him to the Inquisition when he published his telescopic discoveries in *Siderius Nuncius* in 1610. The Inquisition admonished him not to spread the ideas further. In 1632, when he published his *Dialogue on Two World Systems,* he took the precaution of getting imprimaturs. The Inquisition in Rome nevertheless found him guilty and placed his book on the *Index.* He received the relatively mild punishment of house arrest for the rest of his life.

concerned about challenges to its established views. Some of those challenges came from the rise of Protestantism, and some came out of the findings and speculations of scientists. Among the well-established premises of the church was the long-standing belief, supported by various phrases in the Bible, that the Earth stood still and the Sun moved across the heavens.

Several of Galileo's enemies denounced him to the Catholic Church, and he was summoned to Rome to face possible charges of heresy. Heresy, or disagreement with church doctrine, was a crime punishable by death in Italy, Spain, and elsewhere at the time. After an investigation in which Galileo pointed out that he had not intended to challenge the church's views, he was told that he should not publish any views about the universe that contradicted established teachings on the subject. He signed and accepted the "admonition," a prohibition in fact, and promised to comply.

In 1632, he published, in the form of a debate, a work that explored the controversy. The *Dialogue on Two World Systems,* written in Italian, was widely distributed. The debate in the book between heliocentrism and geocentrism appeared to be simply an objective discussion between two advocates, with a third participant making an independent judgment. The conclusion of the independent judge of the debate was that the traditional view was correct; therefore, the book could be viewed as not challenging the church. In fact, before the *Dialogue* was printed, a couple of church censors read the book, passed on it, and officially stamped it with their seal of approval.

However, Galileo was a bit too clever for his own good. Although he had made the book appear to be formally favoring the traditional view, if one read between the lines, one could see that the arguments in favor of the Copernican (heliocentric, therefore heretical) view came across as better than the Catholic Church's preferred Ptolemaic (geocentric) view. It was clear to many readers that Galileo had tried to outwit the church and the censors and that he had initially gotten away with it.

Galileo was called to Rome again and tried for heresy, as well as for violating his admonition not to advocate his view. After confessing his error, he was convicted and sentenced to house arrest in 1633. For the rest of his life, he was confined to his home. By the standards of the day, he got off lightly, since many convicted of heresy were executed by being burned at the stake or by other gruesome methods. In this way, exploration of space by telescope got off to a risky start.

EXPLORING BY TELESCOPE AFTER GALILEO

Over the following centuries, more astronomers began to use telescopes to expand their knowledge of the universe, making discoveries that were built on the findings of Galileo. Others built improved telescopes that were more compact and had better resolution and focus and higher magnification. By the time that Isaac Newton (1642–1727), an English physicist and mathematician, began to consider the solar system, most astronomers had come to accept the view of Copernicus and Galileo that the planets revolved around the Sun, and the ideas could be explored without threat of torture or execution.

Newton invented a telescope that had a side aperture and a mirror system that

Isaac Newton worked out the laws of gravity and of motion that explained the mechanical workings of the solar system. *(Library of Congress, Prints and Photographs Division [LC-USZ62-101363])*

allowed for a shorter length tube for the same degree of magnification as a much longer telescope. Telescopes of that design were later called Newtonian telescopes. Even more important, Newton worked out the basic principles of gravity and the laws of motion that explained how the planets revolved without falling from the sky, and how the Earth itself continued in its orbit around the Sun. By 1700, astronomy had not only a theoretical description of the heavens but a set of mechanical explanations provided by Newton that addressed the commonsense problems with the Copernican view.

Over the next 250 years, the exploration of the universe by telescope resulted in one discovery after another. Astronomers who built their own telescopes and their own observatories made many of the discoveries. It is a tradition that continues today with many amateurs who practice rooftop and backyard astronomy.

German-Polish astronomer Johannes Hevelius (1611–87), for example, drew and published the first detailed map of the surface of the Moon in 1647. Jan Hewel, was born in Danzig, Poland, and had Latinized his name, as was the custom among scientists and scholars, to Hevelius. His *Selenographia,* or Moon map, used the astronomical observations he had made from the roof of his own house. Hevelius was no professional astronomer but financed his exploration of space with funds from his work as a beer merchant and city councilor. Hevelius made numerous other observations of stars and comet paths that his wife gathered and published after his death in a work called *Uranographia* in 1690.

FINDING NEW PLANETS

The spacing of the planets from one another and the Sun puzzled these early explorers of space. A German astronomer, Johann Daniel Titius (1729–96), in 1766, proposed a formula that showed a mathematical pattern for the distances between the planets and the Sun. A fellow German, Johann Elert Bode (1747–1826), popularized the formula in 1772 and later. The idea came to be known as the Titius-Bode law, or Bode's law. The Titius-Bode proportion seemed entrancing, and by its calculations, there should have been a planet between Mars and Jupiter and another undiscovered planet orbiting around the Sun at a distance equal to about 19.6 times the distance from the Sun to the Earth. There was no planet between Mars and Jupiter, but there was a group of small objects in orbit there, called asteroids. The discovery of the fairly large asteroid Ceres in 1801 by the Italian astronomer Giuseppe Piazzi (1746–1826) could be taken to fulfill the prediction implicit in the Titius-Bode relationship. Even more exciting was the earlier discovery of the planet Uranus in 1781 by German-born British astronomer William Herschel (1738–1822) somewhat closer to the Sun than the Titius-Bode law would have placed it. It turned out that the Titius-Bode law was not really a law, and that the calculations for locations of planets further out from Saturn did not hold true.

Herschel had discovered Uranus through a systematic survey with a large telescope that he had built himself. He spotted an object that clearly was not a star and at first assumed that he had found a new comet. He later confirmed that it was the seventh planet from the Sun, the first to be discovered by telescope. The other six had all been known since antiquity, found by the first astrologers of Babylon and others who had explored with the naked eye. Once Herschel found Uranus, observers noticed that it is actually bright enough to be identified without the aid of a telescope. With

Life on Other Planets

ASTRONOMERS' HINTS

Nicolaus Copernicus proposed and Galileo Galilei confirmed that other planets were not simply light sources but made of rock and solid like Earth. Scientists speculated almost immediately that there might be life on the other planets, perhaps even intelligent life. In 1593, Italian philosopher Giordano Bruno (1548–1600), who suggested there might be hundreds of other planets with life like Earth, was arrested by the Inquisition. He was tried for heresy and burned at the stake in 1600. But times changed. In 1877, Giovanni Schiaparelli (1835–1910), an Italian astronomer, drew a picture of the surface of Mars, identifying dark streaks on the surface as *canali,* the Italian word for "grooves." As word of his findings spread, they created excitement, since in English, the word *canali* can be translated as "canals." Of course, on Earth, a canal is a human-made feature, not a natural crack or riverbed. For most of the next century, the idea of canals on Mars provided the basis for hundreds of science fiction stories. The concept was popularized by American self-funded astronomer Percival Lowell, who strongly believed that Mars was inhabited. The human race was eager to believe that on this nearby planet, there were fellow intelligent beings, who would either visit Earth soon or soon be visited by humans.

Other astronomers had trouble spotting the canals that Schiaparelli had seen and that Lowell sought. Most professional astronomers concluded by the 1930s that the lines seen by Schiaparelli were optical effects, not true markings on the surface. However, all agreed that Mars had some interesting features that could conceivably support life, including white ice caps at the northern and southern poles that grew and receded with the seasons. Someday, science fiction fans believed humans would meet the Martians.

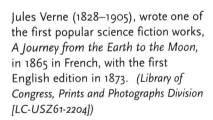

Jules Verne (1828–1905), wrote one of the first popular science fiction works, *A Journey from the Earth to the Moon,* in 1865 in French, with the first English edition in 1873. *(Library of Congress, Prints and Photographs Division [LC-USZ61-2204])*

the unaided eye, it can be seen as a faint speck, but it was just so obscure and small to the eye that no one had noticed its motion against the background of stars before. Herschel planned to name his discovery Georgium Sidus, or Georgian star, after King George III of England, while others thought that the planet should be named in the discoverer's honor. Bode himself suggested the name Uranus for the mythological figure who was the father of Saturn. The name stuck.

Herschel also discovered the two largest satellites of Uranus—Titania and Oberon—in 1787. In other discoveries, Herschel found two moons of Saturn, and he began a method of statistical astronomy, building up star counts for different parts of the night sky. In addition, this telescope-explorer proved that the Sun itself was in motion.

Astronomers working on the mechanics of the orbit of Uranus calculated that it was perturbed by the presence of another large, undiscovered planet. These calculations led, in 1846, to the discovery of the planet Neptune by German astronomer Johann G. Galle (1812–1910). The voyage of exploration and discovery by mathematical calculation leading to finding Neptune was often treated as one of the great accomplishments of 19th-century celestial mechanics, following the principles set forth by Newton. In Berlin, Galle made the first actual sighting of the planet, using his telescope as well as the calculations.

On September 23, 1846, Galle and his colleague, Heinrich d'Arrest (1822–75), also German, located the planet astronomically within an hour of beginning their experiment. They compared their sightings to a printed star map. The planet was less than one degree from the predicted location. One of the ironies is that the astronomers combined Newtonian physics with the Titius-Bode calculations (which turned out to be a false idea), and the discovery of Neptune may have been a lucky accident. In a way, it was parallel to the accidental discovery of the New World by Columbus when his incorrect calculations had led him to assume he had found Asia by sailing to the west.

As telescopes became larger and more expensive, new ones were built by institutions and universities, and the distinction between professional astronomers and amateurs became more pronounced. However, both the hobbyist and the full-time, paid astronomers continued to explore and make discoveries. One who crossed the line between amateur and professional was Percival Lowell (1855–1916), an American, who spent some of his personal fortune in building an observatory in Flagstaff, Arizona, in 1894. As the Italian astronomer Giovanni Schiaparelli (1835–1910) had thought he had seen canals on Mars, Lowell did too. But Lowell went further, developing a whole theory of a system of irrigation canals carrying water from the polar regions to cities in the desert. Alfred Wallace (1823–1913), a respected British engineer and naturalist, challenged Lowell's view, showing that the temperatures on Mars were well below the freezing point of water and that the atmosphere was too thin for Earthlike life. Later spacecraft exploration proved Wallace right and Lowell wrong.

One of the greatest advances in the frontier of space came with a professional American astronomer, Edward Hubble (1889–1953), who discovered that beyond Earth's galaxy (the Milky Way) were thousands of other galaxies, each made up of many stars. Working first at the Yerkes Observatory near Chicago and then at Mount Wilson in California, he introduced in 1925 a classification of the galaxies as different types: spirals, barred spirals, and ellipticals. Hubble also calculated that the universe was expanding.

By the time Hubble published his theories, Russian, German, and American engineers began the first experiments with rockets that would have the potential to visit outer space. The next stage of space exploration was about to begin.

3

FIRST STEPS TO SPACE
Goddard, Peenemunde, and Sputnik

 Although solid-fueled rockets have existed as weapons since their invention in China in the 12th century A.D., the use of rockets for the exploration of space was a 20th-century invention. In the short span of about 30 years, from the mid-1920s through the mid-1950s, the concept of rocket propulsion for spaceships moved from the imaginations of science fiction writers to the reality of engineers' drawing boards and full-scale production.

Both amateurs and professionals played key roles in the rapid series of inventions that resulted in successful rockets that launched payloads into orbit around the Earth and then on their way to the Moon and the other planets of the solar system. Just as in the field of astronomy, it was sometimes hard to distinguish the career of an amateur from that of a professional. The first rocket designers were an interesting assortment. They included high school mathematics teachers, filmmakers and writers, enthusiastic mechanics, unemployed engineers from a wide variety of disciplines, and army artillery officers. At first, there were only a few scientists with graduate degrees in physics and other fields involved in rocketry.

These groups of rocket enthusiasts moved from forming clubs and societies to working with government assistance, and then developing a recognized profession—all in one short generation. Out of these developments grew several corporations in the United States (and later in France and other countries) that manufactured rockets for space exploration. In the Soviet Union, state agencies formed out of the same kind of backgrounds, pioneering the way to space by the 1950s.

EARLY SOVIET AND GERMAN DREAMERS AND PIONEERS

Konstantin Tsiolkovsky (1857–1935) was one of the first advocates of space travel by rocket. He worked as a high school math teacher in a provincial Russian town of Kaluga, about 100 miles from Moscow, but had planned rockets as early as 1895. In 1898, he published the first of three articles in an obscure Russian scientific journal, suggesting how to build such rockets. One of his works, "Exploration of Cosmic Space by Reactive Devices," published in 1903, became the classic piece that foresaw the future of rocket space exploration.

Another math teacher who became interested in space travel was German-speaking, Transylvanian-born Hermann Oberth (1894–1989), who lived in Romania. Oberth began studying rocket propulsion after World War I. He suggested that a rocket propelled by gasoline or kerosene mixed with liquid oxygen would provide far more lift than a rocket fueled by gunpowder or smokeless powder. Thinking ahead, he reasoned that such rockets could put a space station in orbit. He visualized orbiting platforms with huge mirrors that could focus the Sun's rays to melt the ice that locked in some northern ports in the winter. Oberth wrote and published, in 1923, a small pamphlet that summarized his concepts, *Die Rackete zu den Plantenräumen* (The rocket in interplanetary space). Although circulated in limited numbers, his little pamphlet received a lot of notice from some others thinking along the same lines. When Oberth's book came out, Soviet authorities pointed out that Tsiolkovsky had published first, and finally Tsiolkovsky's work received more publicity.

This spurt of interest brought together others in the Soviet Union with similar ideas. Fridrikh Tsander (1887–1933), an engineer from Latvia, began giving lectures on space flight and formed an amateur club, the Society for the Study of Interplanetary Communication, in 1924. Tsander's group of enthusiasts put on a public exhibition in Moscow in 1927, which attracted the attention of Sergei Korolev (1906–66). Korolev had grown fascinated in aviation as a teenager and then attended technical school in Kiev and Moscow. He met Tsiolkovsky in 1927 and Tsander in 1930. Together with Tsander, Korolev helped found in Moscow the Moscow Group for the Study of Reaction Motion (Mos-GIRD). Members joked that the Russian initials of the group also stood for Moscow Group of Engineers Working for Nothing.

Meanwhile, the Soviet army had become interested in rockets, and rocket scientist Valentin Glushko (1908–89) set up an army research group, the Gas Dynamics Laboratory, in Leningrad (now St. Petersburg). In 1932, Glushko built the first liquid rocket engine to fire successfully, burning gasoline and liquid oxygen and producing 44 pounds of thrust. Soon the army also began sending funds to support the work of the GIRD group in Moscow. In 1933, a GIRD rocket climbed to 1,300 feet before crashing. Later that year GIRD and the Leningrad laboratory combined efforts, and the GIRD group moved out of their borrowed basement into a true test facility in a former diesel engine factory outside Moscow. Korolev joined the army and was made an officer.

Meanwhile, efforts in Germany and the United States went forward. In Germany, as in the Soviet Union, independent enthusiasts and amateurs started the effort and later received some government funding. Austrian movie producer Fritz Lang (later famous for many movies including *M* and *The Big Heat*) decided to make a science fiction movie, *Frau im Mond* (*Girl in the Moon*). He hired Oberth as a technical consultant. To promote the movie, Oberth convinced Lang that he should fund the construction of a real rocket. An engineer-promoter by the name of Rudolf Nebel (1894–1978) joined the team. Others criticized Nebel because he often played up meager achievements to win support. Oberth worked with a club, the Verein fur Raumshiffahrt

Wernher von Braun

Wernher Magnus Maximilian von Braun's personal career reflected the typical pathway of rocket scientists from dreamer-visionaries, through military weapons engineering, to the beginnings of space travel. Von Braun was born in Wirsitz, Germany (now in Poland), in 1912 and studied in Berlin and in Zurich, Switzerland. In 1930, he joined a group of rocket enthusiasts in Germany and then was recruited by the German army and encouraged to continue his education. In 1938, he was appointed technical director of a secret facility on the North Sea at Peenemunde, working under the administrative control of General Walter Dornberger. There, the two developed the A-4 rocket, later dubbed the V-2.

In March 1944, von Braun was arrested by the Gestapo, or German secret police, because, it was said, he spent too much time talking about space travel, thereby sabotaging work on the rocket as a weapon. On the insistence of Dornberger, von Braun was released. Dornberger explained that almost everyone connected with Peenemunde could not help but think of the V-2 as a first step in the rocket exploration of space.

At the end of World War II, von Braun and most of his senior staff sought to avoid being captured by the advancing Soviet army, and they moved westward to surrender to U.S. forces. His whole team went to Texas and then worked with the U.S. Army Ordnance Corps at White Sands, New Mexico, to demonstrate the V-2. He became the director of the space flight center at Huntsville, Alabama, with 120 members of the original V-2 team. There, von Braun directed work on the Redstone and Jupiter rockets, as well as *Juno II*. The *Juno II* lifted early deep-space probes, *Pioneer III* and *IV*, as well as

(VfR, or Society for Space Travel), that raised funds. Eventually the German army noticed the efforts run by Oberth and Nebel and provided some small grants.

The VfR recruited dedicated individuals with all sorts of background, including the young aristocrat Wernher von Braun (1912–77), whose father was the last in a long line of barons and whose mother was an enthusiastic amateur astronomer. Von Braun joined Nebel's group and began studies toward a doctorate with army support. By 1934, with army funding, von Braun and colleagues from

the VfR built the A-1 rocket. According to von Braun, it took a half year to build and a half second to blow up. However, the team kept at it and launched an A-2 that flew in December 1934 up to one mile in altitude. In 1936, after discussing the need for a new test range with his family, von Braun convinced the army to support the building of an elaborate test facility on the Baltic Sea at Peenemunde, an isolated spot where his father used to go duck hunting.

Each von Braun design was an improvement over the other, culminating in the A-4,

Explorer satellites. Von Braun worked directly for the National Aeronautics and Space Administration (NASA) from 1970 to 1972, and he died at age 65 in 1977.

Wernher von Braun headed the team of German engineers who moved to the United States after World War II to help develop rockets. Behind him is the *Saturn IB*, built under his direction, ready for launch at the Kennedy Space Flight Center in Florida. Saturn rockets were used in many U.S. space programs. *(NASA)*

which had a system of changing the direction of thrust of the motors. Flanges in the rocket exhaust turned, controlled by a gyroscope, to keep the rocket at a steady angle despite variations in winds aloft. It was said to be like trying to balance a stick on the back of one's hand, but the A-4 worked.

During World War II, the German dictator Adolf Hitler realized the potential of the rocket to carry a heavy explosive payload directly to London and other targets. He ordered General Walter Dornberger to put the weapon in production. The propaganda minister Joseph Goebbels named the von Braun–designed A-4 rocket the Vengeance Weapon 2, or V-2. The research, development, and manufacture of the weapons while being bombed by the Allies was slow and difficult work. The first V-2 rockets were launched only nine months before the defeat of Germany. The Germans fired more than 3,700 V-2s during the last months of the war, each carrying a one-ton warhead. Many were aimed at Allied-occupied Antwerp, Belgium, and others landed in London. The weapons could not be precisely aimed, and they often knocked out farmland, or residential or commercial sections. Only sometimes did they hit a strategic target like a factory, railroad yard, or bridge.

PRISONERS AND REFUGEES

The period of rocket development during World War II (1939–45) was one of international crisis and political repression; therefore, during that period, many of the amateurs-turned-professionals and associated workers often found themselves in prisons. In the Soviet Union, many of the key rocket developers, including Korolev and Glushko, were rounded up by Joseph Stalin's secret police and sent off to labor camps, along with millions of others, most completely innocent of any crime. But the head of the Soviet police, Lavrenti Beria, realized that, even if some of the engineers and others were "politically unreliable," they represented a key asset for the Soviet state. So the best minds were collected and sent to special prison camps known as *sharagas,* where Beria put them to work designing long-range rockets.

In Germany, prisoners (mostly political and ethnic victims of the Nazi regime) did the manual labor for making the V-2 rockets. Such slave labor staffed the factory at Nordhausen that produced the rockets, and forced labor did much of the construction at Peenemunde on the Baltic Sea. The same SS officers who ran the notorious death camps, such as Auschwitz and Buchenwald, managed the prisoner rocket work, some at the Dora prison camp, a branch of Buchenwald. (The SS was a special political police that served the Nazi party, not only running the death camps, but also using terror tactics to intimidate or murder opponents of the regime.)

At the end of the war, both the United States and the Soviet Union wanted to learn how to make the V-2 rockets. V-2 engineers and technicians were hired and transferred to both countries. The United States and the Soviet Union recruited the technical people with offers of pay and interesting work, and most of them took the new jobs, because if they had stayed in Germany, none of them would have been able to continue in their careers in the rocket business. Both the United States and the Soviet Union were able, within a short span of a decade, to build new generations of rockets applying the V-2 principles for rockets capable of reaching into the fringes of outer space.

UNITED STATES: Robert Goddard and Others

Earlier, through the 1920s and 1930s, Americans had also worked on liquid-fueled rockets, but without much support from the government. The key researcher in the United States was Robert Goddard (1882–1945). As a teenager, in 1899, he read the novel by H. G. Wells *War of the Worlds,* in which Martians invaded the Earth. Goddard studied physics and attended Clark University, where he earned a doctorate studying under Nobel Prize winner Albert Michelson. Goddard won a research grant from the Smithsonian Institution and produced a short pamphlet in 1920 entitled *A Method of Reaching Extreme Altitudes.* In this 69-page booklet, he calculated the escape velocity and thrust needed to lift a rocket off the surface of the Earth. He also calculated that it could be crashed into the Moon, with a charge of flash powder that could be seen from Earth to verify the successful flight. The idea caught the imagination of newspaper writers, and Goddard was soon popularized as the "Moon Man" in newspapers across the United States.

H. G. Wells (1866–1946) carried on the science fiction tradition begun by Jules Verne, with his *War of the Worlds*, predicting a Martian invasion of Earth, published in 1898, and *The First Men on the Moon*, in 1901. *(Library of Congress, Prints and Photographs Division [LC-USZ62-119873])*

and helped him arrange a grant from the Guggenheim Foundation. The money was enough for Goddard to move to New Mexico and set up a small laboratory of his own together with a test facility outside Roswell. He kept working on rockets and getting patents on gyroscopic controls and other aspects of the system. In fact, in Germany, von Braun collected available copies of the U.S. patents that included detailed drawings and explanations, and he freely admitted later that some of the ideas for the early A-series rockets and the eventual V-2 were drawn from Goddard's publicly available patents.

Robert Goddard patented several techniques and devices for stabilizing liquid-fueled rockets in flight. Although he never built large rockets, his ideas anticipated many of the details later used in the German V-2 rockets built by Wernher von Braun. *(NASA)*

Goddard was naturally shy and the sensational publicity shocked him. He became more reclusive but continued to work on rocket projects. He developed a liquid-fueled rocket in 1926 (before the similar German and Soviet projects), but his first rocket flew less than 200 feet. As a physicist, he was not a great mechanic, and he tended to work alone, often on small models to test out principles.

Even so, his ideas attracted interest. One day in 1929, he got a phone call from Charles Lindbergh, who was already internationally famous for his solo trans-Atlantic flight in 1927. Lindbergh listened to Goddard's ideas

Among Robert Goddard's first experiments, this small rocket made one of the first successful flights by a liquid-fueled rocket in 1926, in Auburn, Massachusetts. Goddard used liquid oxygen and gasoline. *(NASA)*

As a loner, Goddard stayed away from others in the United States who worked on rocket development. A group in New York, formed by editors and writers of the science fiction magazine *Science Wonder Stories,* set up an organization called the American Interplanetary Society. Soon they changed the name to the less fanciful title the American Rocket Society (ARS). As was the case for similar groups in Moscow and Berlin, the club lacked funds and consisted of enthusiastic amateurs together with a few unemployed mechanics, technicians, and engineers who dreamed of space travel. The ARS arranged a showing of Lang's *Girl in the Moon,* attracting a huge audience and gaining a few new members.

With a small budget and borrowed tools, the group arranged rocket tests on Staten Island, New York, and later at a more open space in New Jersey. Their work attracted a Princeton student, James Wyld (1913–53). He finished his college degree and began building rockets. Wyld and another ARS member, Lovell Lawrence (1915–71), were able to convince the U.S. Navy to support their work, but only if the two would form a company. They set up Reaction Motors, Incorporated and began to work on navy contracts. The company later merged with Thiokol Chemical Corporation.

During World War II, the meager beginnings of American rocketry began to expand. Goddard went to the Annapolis Marine Engineering Laboratory, where he worked under Robert Truax on jet-assisted takeoff, or JATO, rockets. A few months before his death from cancer in 1945, Goddard inspected a captured V-2 rocket. He studied it closely. A colleague, who knew his work, was curious and asked if it did not seem the V-2 parts resembled Goddard's own ideas. Quietly, Goddard admitted, so it seemed.

In Pasadena, at the California Institute of Technology (Caltech), a professor of aeronautic engineering, Theodor von Kármán (1881–1963), originally from Hungary, collected a group of scientists to work on rockets. Some came from facilities such as the U.S. Navy's Ordnance Station at Indian Head, Maryland, and other facilities, and they began testing rockets in a dry arroyo in the hills near the campus of Caltech. As the California academics began work on war projects, they formed a special unit of the institute to take on defense research work, the Jet Propulsion Laboratory. Some of them later went on to form the company Aerojet General.

Seated in front is Hermann Oberth, and behind him, to the right, is Wernher von Braun, two of the many German rocket enthusiasts brought to America after World War II. They are pictured here at the Army Ballistic Missile Agency at Huntsville, Alabama, with other members of their team. *(NASA)*

FOLLOWING UP ON THE V-2

When the war ended, both the Soviet Union and the United States tried to round up parts and complete V-2 rockets, together with the scientists, engineers, and technicians who had worked on them. The United States was able to bring back, across the Atlantic, numerous complete rockets and most of the top technical people; the Soviets established contact with one or two factories that had made components, as well as many of the lower-level technicians. So in 1945, both countries began to build directly on the V-2 experience.

In the United States, von Braun and some 120 others from his Peenemunde group moved first to Fort Bliss, Texas, and began testing and demonstrating V-2 rockets at White Sands, New Mexico, not far from where the United States had tested its first nuclear weapon in July 1945. In 1946–47, several projects went forward at the same time, with

This modified German V-2 was launched at Cape Canaveral, Florida, in 1950. In the foreground, camera crews record the performance. (NASA)

funding from different branches of the U.S. military. Later, von Braun and his group moved to Huntsville, Alabama, and worked at the Redstone Arsenal there.

In this prolific period of studying the V-2 and sharing research and ideas, engineers made several new U.S. rockets. The Jet Propulsion Laboratory developed the WAC Corporal in 1947 for the U.S. Army, with an engine built by Reaction Motors. By 1949, a WAC Corporal rocket reached a height of 244 miles, a record held until 1956. The navy paid for studies that led to a successful flight of the Viking rocket in 1954. The Viking took one of the first pictures of Earth from outer space, showing the curvature out over the Pacific Ocean. The U.S. Air Force contracted with North American Aviation, which hired some of von Braun's staff. Building on the V-2 experience, they designed a winged rocket known as the Navaho. The Navaho engines produced 75,000 pounds of thrust compared to the V-2's 56,000 pounds.

SPUTNIK

During the International Geophysical Year, from July 1957 to December 1958, the United States anticipated launching a satellite, seeking to use a nonmilitary rocket, the Vanguard, rather than the larger Jupiter rocket being developed at the Redstone Arsenal in Alabama by the von Braun team to boost an intercontinental ballistic missile (ICBM). The Soviet Union, rival of the United States in the cold war, won the race to launch a satellite successfully. The Soviets put the satellite *Sputnik 1* in orbit around the Earth on October 4, 1957. The team, headed by Korolev, worked from a well-financed cosmodrome in the Soviet republic of Kazakhstan.

In Russian, *sputnik* means "fellow traveler." The name had a double meaning: First, the satellite accompanied Earth in its travels

Sergei Korolev, one of the founders of the Soviet space program, shows off a dog that flew successfully in 1954 to a height of 100 kilometers. *(NASA)*

around the Sun; second, the term was a play on words on the political phrase that referred to a nonparty supporter of the communist ideology. Around the world, teams of volunteers had been established to track satellites, so the Soviets installed aboard *Sputnik* a radio beacon broadcasting on ham radio frequencies, that made radio tracking a lot easier. A month after *Sputnik 1*, on November 3, 1957, the Soviets launched *Sputnik 2,* which carried a dog named Laika aboard.

American politicians, journalists, and the public were stunned. Although the Soviets had announced in advance the plans to launch a satellite, most Americans scoffed at the claims as propaganda. The American public had no idea that the Soviets had been working on rockets since the 1920s, and most had never heard of Korolev, Glushko, and Tsander. The press reports on the transfer of the von Braun team to the United States made people think the country was far ahead of any competition from the Soviet Union.

Quietly, the Soviets had already developed a large military rocket for carrying ICBMs with heavy payloads of nuclear weapons. Stalin had insisted that in order to meet the threat posed by the U.S. capability to carry nuclear weapons by long-range bomber aircraft, the rocket engineers should push forward in designing a rocket capable of carrying a heavy nuclear weapon all the way to the United States. Korolev led construction of the R-7 rocket, which he powered with a cluster of 20 liquid-oxygen-and-kerosene-fueled engines. The R-7 met Stalin's need for an ICBM rocket and it could also launch satellites.

Sputnik 1 initiated the "space race" between the Soviet Union and the United States in earnest. Investigations soon revealed that the U.S. military Jupiter rocket could easily launch a satellite, so a Jupiter booster lifted the first U.S. satellite, *Explorer 1,* into orbit on January 31, 1958. The first successful Vanguard launch was March 17, 1958. Exploration of space by rocket—born out of military competition but inspired by a generation of amateurs and dreamers—had begun.

4

ASTRONAUTS AND COSMONAUTS

 Human space exploration, like earlier rocket development, grew out of the military confrontation between the major world powers. At the end of World War II, American and Soviet rocket programs drew heavily on the German experience in building the V-2. In 1945, with the dropping of the atomic bomb in Hiroshima and Nagasaki, the United States showed the world that it had developed nuclear weapons and was capable of using them in warfare. Almost immediately, military experts and the general public alike saw the link to the wartime development of warhead-carrying rockets like the V-2. If nuclear weapons could be carried aboard long-distance or especially aboard intercontinental rockets, any nation could be put at risk of sudden nuclear devastation. Rockets that could leave the Earth were first used, not for exploration, but as potential weapons. That had been true of the V-2, and it remained true of the rockets built through the 1950s and early 1960s.

Both the Soviet Union and the United States sought to impress other countries that their respective social and economic systems were superior. Both competed for influence in nonaligned countries in Africa and Asia. Achievements in space by the Soviet Union or the United States might have had little to do with prosperity on Earth, but they did serve a propaganda purpose: If one nation or the other pulled ahead in technological achievements, nonaligned peoples would tend to believe that the winning nation had a system that produced results and therefore was better. Superior technology and superior achievements in space could influence millions of people around the world. So the propaganda side of the cold war, as well as the arms race, could have an impact on space flight development.

ATOMIC WEAPONS AND ICBMS

Developed in a secret program known as the Manhattan Project, the first atomic bombs were far more powerful than any weapon ever

37

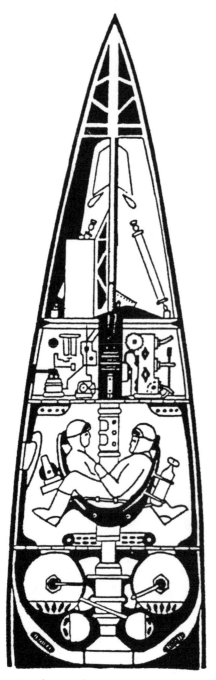

The Russians began planning to put a person in space over a decade before they actually tried it, as this 1945 conceptual drawing shows. *(NASA)*

seen before. The United States tested its first bomb in secret at a test site in New Mexico on July 16, 1945. Then, less than a month later, two atomic bombs were dropped, the first on Hiroshima, Japan, on August 6, 1945, and the second on August 8, 1945, on another Japanese city, Nagasaki. Although exact casualty figures remained in dispute, the two weapons killed about 300,000 people, mostly civilians. Realizing that their nation faced devastation, the Japanese accepted Allied terms for unconditional surrender on August 15, and they formally signed the surrender documents September 2, 1945, that ended World War II.

Although the Soviet Union had maintained a number of spies in the United States who kept the Soviet leader Joseph Stalin well posted on nuclear research, the Soviets had not poured resources into the potential weapon during World War II. However, once the United States had long-range aircraft capable of reaching many cities in the Soviet Union, Stalin ordered his nuclear scientists, headed by Igor Kurchatov (1903–60), to accelerate research and development on an atomic bomb, following the American design, which had been obtained through spies. He also ordered Sergei Korolev and Valentin Glushko, the Soviet Union's leading rocket developers, to improve on the V-2 to provide a rocket that would be capable of carrying a nuclear weapon from a base in the Soviet Union to the United States. Just as the cold war of political and diplomatic tensions between the United States and the Soviet Union began, it was accompanied by an arms race, much of it conducted in secret.

Although there were signs of tension between the United States and the Soviet Union earlier, the cold war itself is usually dated from 1948. A year later, in August 1949, the Soviet Union tested its first atomic bomb, known to the West as "Joe 1" after Joseph Stalin. Soon, the British and Americans learned that the secret Manhattan Project had been thoroughly penetrated by spies. One spy in particular, Klaus Fuchs, a German refugee who had taken on British citizenship and then worked on the Manhattan Project in the United States, confessed in 1950 to spying for the Soviets. He had provided his Russian spymasters with detailed drawings and specially written reports that allowed the Soviet program to move quickly forward to its first bomb.

The Soviet Union lacked long-range bombers capable of carrying atomic bombs to the United States, while American bombers based in Western Europe could easily strike Soviet cities. The threat of a retaliation attack, American military planners believed, would prevent any aggressive Soviet action, because American response would lead to destruction of Soviet cities. Even so, the United States went ahead to develop a more powerful thermonuclear weapon—the hydrogen bomb, or H-bomb—that was so destructive it could thoroughly destroy a city and its surrounding region. Meanwhile, the Soviet Union also developed a similar weapon, testing it within about a year of the first American test.

COLD WAR AND MISSILE ACHIEVEMENTS

In the face of such horrible weapons of mass destruction, the cold war intensified, and the two nations and their groups of allied nations worried that a crisis over some local issue such as Soviet influence in East Germany or Hungary could escalate into a full-fledged war. Yet many military strategists in the United States believed during the 1950s that the Soviet Union would lag far behind in rocket development. After all, many of the leading German rocket designers who had built the V-2, including Wernher von Braun, had immigrated to the United States after the war. Considering that the Russians had used stolen plans to develop their first atomic bomb, analysts believed that the Soviets would lag behind in rockets capable of carrying a nuclear or thermonuclear weapon around the world to the United States.

However, in 1957, when *Sputnik I* was launched, and its radio beam was picked up by ham radio receivers around the world, the balance of nuclear terror suddenly seemed to shift. A rocket capable of putting a satellite in an Earth-circling orbit would be capable of

Soviet Union and Russians

The Soviet Union, established out of the Russian Empire at the end of World War I (1918), formally consisted of a union of 15 different republics, the largest of which was Russia. Although each of the republics maintained its own language, such as Lithuanian, Georgian, and Ukrainian, the Russian language was widely used throughout the Soviet Union. During the period of the cold war between the Soviet Union and the United States of America, Americans often erroneously called all Soviet citizens "Russians"; for most of the public and the popular news media, the terms *Russia* and *Soviet Union* were used almost interchangeably.

Publicity about several unsuccessful efforts to launch a Vanguard rocket, like this one blowing up on the pad in 1957, helped contribute to U.S. insecurities about the Soviet lead in rockets and missiles. *(NASA, U.S. Navy)*

carrying a weapon all the way from one continent to another. Thus, Sputnik proved that the Soviets could build an intercontinental ballistic missile, or ICBM. (It was termed *ballistic* because it was not guided during its flight but only aimed at the beginning of its flight like an artillery piece or cannon, flying in a ballistic arc out of the atmosphere and then returning by gravity and momentum to its target.)

In the United States, the reaction to Sputnik began with initial popular disbelief that the "backward Russians" could develop such a technological marvel but soon turned to panic. By 1958, Americans began to fear the Soviet Union had gotten ahead in the arms race. New programs funding higher education and stimulating research flowed out of Washington, D.C., and politicians talked of a possible "missile gap," meaning that the United States had fallen behind in missile development, and the Soviets had pulled ahead. To the Soviet leaders, it was more important that the Americans and their allies believe the Soviets were ahead, than it was to be actually ahead.

By boasting about their missile strength, the Soviets fed the idea that there was a missile gap. By 1960, public opinion in the United States, Britain, France, and other Western European countries had definitely shifted. Polls showed that many more people believed the Soviets were ahead of the United States in military strength and that their lead would grow in the future. The Soviets kept much of their program secret, including the location of the launch sites, the names of the scientists involved, and the statistics of money spent and personnel assigned. All of the secrecy only fed anxiety further among Europeans and Americans.

In order to find out whether there was indeed a missile gap, President Dwight Eisenhower authorized secret high-altitude aircraft flights by Central Intelligence Agency U-2 aircraft to take pictures of possible Soviet missile installations. When the Soviets shot down one of these U.S. spy planes on May 1, 1960, the secret mission was revealed. Although the photographs did not show a tremendous ICBM arsenal, the information might be incomplete. Americans' intelligence officials had to wait until images began to flow from photoreconnaissance satellites some months later before they could be sure that the Soviet ICBM lead was not a real threat to U.S. security.

Meanwhile, the Soviet program of launching satellites and beginning preparations for manned space travel went forward. In 1958, Korolev converted an obsolete aircraft factory near Moscow into a "manned space flight center." The fact that the Americans were beginning a manned program known as Project Mercury in 1958 spurred on the Soviets. The Soviet program was known as Vostok, meaning "the east," although it could also mean "upward flow." The name choice was to suggest that the progress of the human race came from the Soviets, not from the West.

COSMONAUT VS. ASTRONAUT: The Race for Space

The Soviets called their spacecraft pilots "cosmonauts" while the Americans planned to put "astronauts" in space. By 1958, an offshoot of the cold war and the arms race became the race to put a cosmonaut or astronaut in space first.

The two plans were slightly different. The Soviet Vostok plan was to send a man aloft and have him orbit the Earth, then drop through the atmosphere in a capsule and parachute to the ground with a personal harness parachute. The American Mercury plan was to shoot a man into space on a rocket in a long arc, with him being returned down range to the sea in a parachute-slowed capsule about 300 miles from the launch site. While not an orbit, the launching of the first "man in space" might help in the propaganda war with the Soviet Union over doing things first. A simple arc, while not as impressive as an orbit around the world, would count as putting a man in space and bringing him home safely.

Through 1959–61, both countries had some failures in their projects. The U.S. Army had developed a long-range Jupiter rocket, and it was used to carry two monkeys, named Able and Baker on a suborbital trajectory into near space in May 1959. The Redstone rocket held out promise for a longer flight, but when mated to a Mercury capsule capable of carrying a man, the test shot in November 1960 failed. The Mercury-Redstone match-up was known as the MR series. On December 19, 1960, the empty MR-1A did all right, reaching an altitude of 131 miles. MR-2, carrying a chimpanzee named Ham, went up on January 31, 1961. Ham survived the flight, despite a few mistakes, such as landing in the ocean some 130 miles beyond the target zone. He had to wait over two hours, bobbing around in the Atlantic Ocean, before rescuers arrived. Although he seemed perfectly happy when brought aboard, engineers worried that MR-2 had not flown according to plan.

Seven human astronauts stood ready to volunteer to go into space on the first available MR. Concerned with safety, NASA decided to test the MR system one more time to make sure it was "man rated" or capable of safely carrying a human being into space. On March 24, 1961, another MR without anyone aboard flew successfully and splashed down right on target.

Meanwhile, Korolev worked with the Vostok team, keeping close tabs on the highly publicized American program. On April 12, 1961, Korolev fired up a modified ICBM, with Yuri Alekseyevich Gagarin aboard. Gagarin completed one orbit around the world in 90 minutes, landing by parachute in a pasture in central Russia. The Russians were happy to announce that Gagarin landed safely on a collective farm named for V. I. Lenin, not far from one town named Karl Marx and another named Friedrich Engels. Thus the Russians won the race to put the first human in space, and they were able to make good propaganda out of the fact, by landing near places named for important communist figures.

American specialists were disappointed. Navy commander Alan Bartlett Shepard had been ready and willing to go into his suborbital flight in March, several weeks before the Russian shot. The empty test MR vehicle could have carried him; instead, he flew down range on May 5, 1961, in a tiny spacecraft named *Freedom 7*. Launched from Cape Canaveral, Florida, Shepard reached an altitude of 115 miles. A few days later, President John Kennedy presented Shepard with a Distinguished Service Medal before he rode in an open-car parade down Pennsylvania Avenue in the capital. Kennedy was impressed with Shepard and excited by the whole space competition. The fact that Gagarin got to space a few weeks earlier than Shepard would only spur further competition. As the first men in space, Gagarin and Shepard became not only heroes in their respective countries, but symbols for the world of the competition between the two nations.

Only much later did news leak about a major accident in the Soviet secret space program, much worse than any of the minor setbacks that had troubled the Americans. Under Premier Nikita Khrushchev, the Soviets had hoped to score an even bigger success

The Mercury capsules that took the first Americans into space were little more than small protective shells. *(NASA, Ernie Walker)*

Final stage shutdown,
orbit insertion at 676 seconds

Begin orientation for retro burn at
8000 km from landing site
at 9:51 MT

Retro burn and instrument
module seperation at 10:25 MT
begin reentry at 10:35 MT

Jettison core stage,
final stage ignition
at 300 seconds

Jettison hatch at 7,000 meters
cosmonaut ejects 2 seconds
later at 10:55 MT

Jettison hatch at 4,000 meters
and deploy braking chute

Jettison shroud at
156 seconds

Separates strap-on
stages at 119 seconds

Deploy main chute
at 2,500 meters

Cosmonaut separates
from seat at 4,000 meters

Launch from Baikonur
Kosmodrome at Leninsk
at 9:07 MT

Cosmonaut lands in Saratov region at 11:05 MT

Takeoff

Reentry

that would impress the world in 1960. They had planned to send an unmanned rocket to Mars in October 1960, timed to be announced when Khrushchev visited the United Nations in New York City. However, two rockets fizzled out after leaving their launchpads on October 10 and 14. Then on October 23, a third rocket failed to ignite. The head of the Soviet Strategic Rocket Forces, Marshal Mitrovan Nedelin, ordered technicians out of their protective blockhouses to examine the rocket and find out the cause. As they approached, the propellants in the rocket exploded, killing many of the engineers and technicians. The exact number was never released. Korolev was inside a protective building, but Nedelin himself died. It was nearly 20 years before the Soviet officials admitted that Nedelin had been killed in the accident.

Korolev's successful launch of *Vostok 1* in April 1961 with Gagarin aboard together with the success of the Soviets in keeping their bad accident a secret convinced world opinion that the Soviet Union had made great achievements. Despite Shepard's flight and doubts about the honesty of Soviet claims, polls around the world continued to show that most people believed the Soviets were far ahead of the Americans in the competition for space.

The technical side of the race, as distinct from the propaganda side, was another story. Later analysts have concluded that the Russian equipment was poorly designed. Khrushchev claimed that the achievements of Gagarin proved that the Soviet technology had pulled ahead of American and Western technology and that its benefits would flow to the Soviet people. However, Soviet rocketry had been a force-fed development in a military economy. It depended on shifting resources away from needed development in

In 1965, Alexei Leonov was the first person to do an extravehicular activity, or space walk, as captured on this Soviet movie film. *(NASA)*

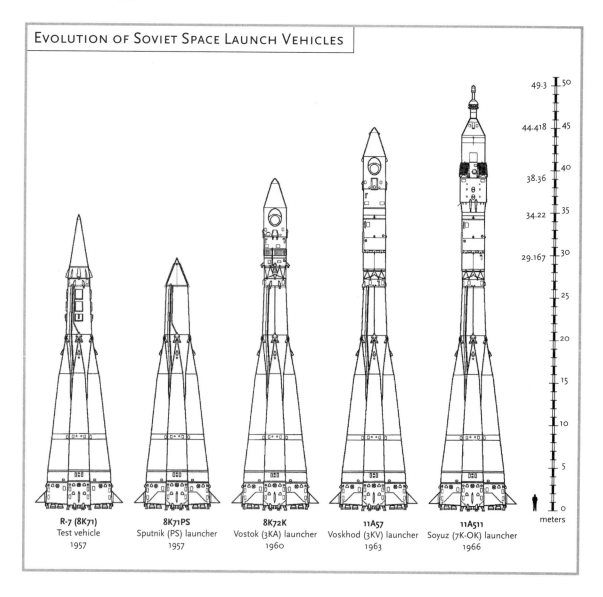

EVOLUTION OF SOVIET SPACE LAUNCH VEHICLES

49.3 — 50

44.418 — 45

40

38.36

34.22 — 35

29.167 — 30

25

20

15

10

5

0

meters

R-7 (8K71)
Test vehicle
1957

8K71PS
Sputnik (PS) launcher
1957

8K72K
Vostok (3KA) launcher
1960

11A57
Voskhod (3KV) launcher
1963

11A511
Soyuz (7K-OK) launcher
1966

light manufacturing, consumer goods, and agriculture. Ironically, what Khrushchev was advertising to the world as proof of Soviet progress really came at a price that held that progress back.

For Khrushchev's American counterpart, President John F. Kennedy, the competition had become a burning issue. He was already contemplating the next step in the international space race: a mission to the Moon.

5

THE RACE FOR THE MOON

On May 25, 1961, President John F. Kennedy, in a speech to a joint session of Congress, posed a dramatic challenge to the nation. He proposed that the United States

> should commit itself to achieving the goal, before this decade is out, of landing a man on the moon and returning him safely to earth. No single space project in this period will be more impressive to mankind, or more important for the long-range exploration of space; and none will be so difficult or expensive to accomplish.

The reasons for this astounding statement lay embedded in the nature of the Kennedy presidency. Kennedy at age 43 had campaigned against the administration of Dwight Eisenhower, representing his own team as a new generation, willing to take on new frontiers. Kennedy sought to challenge the Soviet Union for a position of leadership among the nations of the world. However, the recent victory of the Soviets in placing cosmonaut Yuri Gagarin in space three weeks before NASA astronaut Alan Shepard probably represented

the final nudge to action. The motives were summed up in the statement, both to be "impressive to mankind" and to advance the "long-range exploration of space."

Over the next eight and a half years, NASA pushed an expensive and risky program that achieved the goal. In order to meet it, NASA had to navigate two very difficult dilemmas, one technical and the other political.

NASA'S DILEMMAS

Engineers constantly faced the pressure of the schedule at the core of the technical dilemma. The goal of reaching the Moon "before this decade is out" was very explicit. The round trip had to be accomplished before December 31, 1969. That meant that NASA had to pressure designers to come up with workable machines and to constantly press contractors to provide solutions to problems, but not to delay or take extra time while developing the solutions. The difficulty faced by astronauts Jim Lovell, Fred Haise, and Jack Swigert on *Apollo 13* was by no means the only or the worst technical crisis of the program.

Accidents revealed several technical difficulties or mistakes that seemed obvious in retrospect but were overlooked in the rush to meet the schedule. Too great a concern with perfection would delay the program and lead to its "failure" to meet the deadline. The Russian saying "Perfect is the enemy of good enough" seemed to become part of the American approach. On the other hand, too great a concern with the schedule could contribute to accidents that would risk loss of support. Through taking on some risks, and

aiming at systems that performed well and staffing them with brilliant pilots and scientists, NASA found its way. Tragic losses were taken in stride, and shots to the Moon went off with less-than-perfect equipment, that after all, usually could be made to work, accomplishing some, if not all of the expected objectives.

Another dilemma concerned publicity. NASA gained public and political support by surrounding the individual astronauts with a constant barrage of media, making them

On July 20, 1961, President John F. Kennedy challenged the nation, to land a man on the Moon and return him safely to Earth before the decade was out. At left, Vice President Lyndon Johnson, who had recommended such a program, listens intently. *(NASA)*

Accompanied by administrator Robert Seamans *(left)*, Wernher von Braun explains a Saturn launch system to President John F. Kennedy *(right)*. *(NASA)*

heroes in the eyes of the public. The public attention showered on the astronauts seemed to be a deserved recognition of their bravery, but at the same time, the publicity often served as a distraction from their real work. Whenever an accident happened, the intense glare of public attention on the men and their families could backfire and bring with it the risk that the program would suffer closer political scrutiny and perhaps loss of public support. So NASA walked a public affairs tightrope through the decade, at the same time trying (usually successfully) to woo the support of the media and always fearing that slippage of schedule or human tragedy could destroy that support.

UNDERLYING REASONS FOR THE RACE

As Kennedy's vice president, Lyndon Johnson headed the Space Council. In a report to the president before Kennedy's May speech, Johnson listed six reasons why the Moon venture

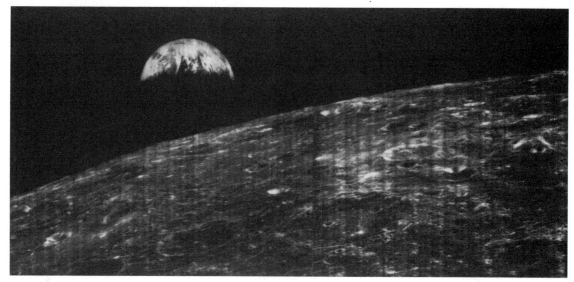

This picture, taken in 1966 by the unmanned *Lunar Orbiter 1*, was the first image of the Earth ever recorded from the vicinity of the Moon. *(NASA)*

should be undertaken; the reasons showed how the goal was an extension of the cold war competition with the Soviet Union. Johnson's reasons were

1. The Soviet Union was ahead in prestige.
2. The United States had so far failed to bring its own superior technical resources to bear on space.
3. Other countries would line up with the country that seemed to be the leader.
4. If the United States failed to take action, the Soviets would extend their lead so far that the United States would not be able to catch up.
5. Even in areas where the Soviets were ahead, the United States should make aggressive efforts.
6. Manned exploration of the Moon was of great propaganda value and was also essential to the advancement of human knowledge.

With the 1961 speech and the Kennedy policies, carried forward by succeeding presidents Johnson (1963–69) and Richard Nixon (1969–74), the United States converted space exploration into a national enterprise, so the job was psychological, organizational, and political, as well as technical.

One delicate issue was the question of the military value of the enterprise. An overemphasis on the military benefits of the space program could result in a falloff in world opinion and support. Thus the effort was mounted through the new NASA civilian agency that had been formed in 1958, rather than through the U.S. Air Force.

To ensure the peaceful program, as defined by the United States, President Johnson signed the international Outer Space Treaty, ratified by the U.S. Senate on February 7, 1967, guaranteeing the peaceful uses of space. The treaty represented exactly the policy the United States endorsed: It declared that there would be no national sovereignty over space (just as there was no national sovereignty over the open oceans). The treaty banned the placement of weapons in outer space. At the same time, it did not prohibit satellites designed to gather military intelligence, did not require that the United States and the Soviet Union or other countries cooperate in space ventures, and did not prohibit the use of military personnel or even military equipment (such as the rockets themselves) in space exploration. Under the treaty, the United States could work out agreements with Australia and Kenya to set up tracking stations to monitor its space vehicles, but such countries would not be required to offer similar facilities to the Soviets.

ASTRONAUTS AS HEROES

NASA encouraged the media in making heroes out of the astronauts in many ways. In 1966 alone, in January through November, astronauts made 810 public appearances and gave 314 formal presentations. The public affairs office handled another 1,600 appearance requests and processed more than 70,000 pieces of correspondence. The astronauts were glad of some of the perks that came with the job, such as the loan of Corvette sports cars by a Florida auto dealer, special reduced rates for themselves and their wives at a luxury resort in Acapulco, and for some, a regular payment from *Life* magazine for articles they prepared. On the other hand, they often resented the limelight, and sometimes even threatened to limp or to mark their faces with

Original Seven and New Nine

The first NASA astronauts were recruited in groups, and soon the press caught on to the names given to the different groups: the Original Seven, who had flown in Mercury missions; the New Nine, many of whom flew on Apollo missions; and other classes of 14 and 19. In all, there were about 50 astronauts in NASA's program between 1962 and 1971. The early astronauts became so well known that the press and American public usually remembered them by their nicknames:

The Original Seven (1959)

Scott Carpenter
Gordo Cooper
John Glenn
Gus Grissom
Wally Schirra
Alan Shepard
Deke Slayton

The New Nine (1962)

Neil Armstrong
Frank Borman
Charles Conrad
Jim Lovell
Jim McDivitt
Elliott See
Thomas Stafford
Edward White
John Young

dye to simulate illness if the public affairs office would not hold back the flood of cameras.

THE GEMINI FLIGHTS

The Gemini series of space flights, held between 1964 and 1966, were two-man flights intended to test a number of navigation and space maneuvers that would be needed for the Apollo missions, including such techniques as docking in space, controlling the flight of a spacecraft to maneuver it into position, and extravehicular activity (EVA), also known as spacewalking. Altogether there were 12 Gemini missions. The first two missions, actually unmanned, demonstrated such objectives as the effectiveness of the heat shield on reentry; the performance of systems and subsystems, ground control, and guidance; and training for the ground controllers.

PROBLEMS ON GEMINI MISSIONS

Mission	Date	Astronauts	Objectives and Problems
Gemini 3	March 23, 1965	Gus Grissom and John Young	demonstrated manned orbital flight; missed splashdown target by 60 miles
Gemini 4	June 3–7, 1965	Jim McDivitt and Edward White	evaluated performance in prolonged flight; missed splashdown target by 44 miles
Gemini 5	Aug. 21–29, 1965	Gordo Cooper and Charles Conrad	evaluated rendezvous system and effect of weightlessness; missed splashdown target by 92 miles
Gemini 6	Dec. 15–16, 1965	Wally Schirra and Thomas Stafford	rendezvous with Gemini 7, which had been rescheduled after propulsion failure in October
Gemini 7	Dec. 4–18, 1965	Frank Borman and Jim Lovell	14-day mission; rendezvous with Gemini 6
Gemini 8	March 16–17, 1966	Neil Armstrong and David Scott	EVA; rendezvous and dock with launch vehicle; mission terminated because of electrical failure
Gemini 9-A	June 3–6, 1966	Thomas Stafford and Gene Cernan	EVA, rendezvous and dock with launch vehicle; had been rescheduled after Atlas failure May 17
Gemini 10	July 18–21, 1966	John Young and Michael Collins	rendezvous and docking practice; docking terminated for high fuel use
Gemini 11	Sept. 12–15, 1966	Charles Conrad and Richard Gordon	rendezvous and docking practice; EVA terminated early
Gemini 12	Nov. 11–15, 1966	Jim Lovell and Buzz Aldrin	rendezvous and docking maneuvers; dock work canceled because of equipment problem

Gemini 9-A splashed down at sea with Eugene Cernan and Thomas Stafford aboard in 1966. *(NASA)*

The other 10 missions proceeded almost on schedule, with now and then a difficulty showing up that caused a delay or only a partial completion of objectives.

As the Gemini list indicates, there were serious technical problems on nearly every mission. In many cases, the returning capsule missed the target area of the ocean. Some

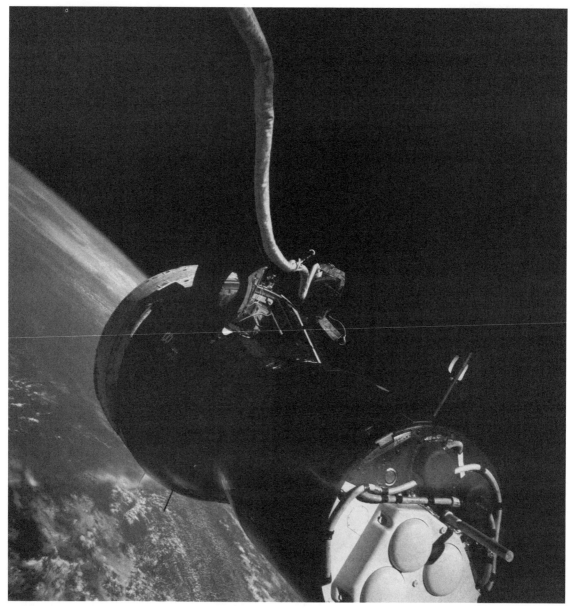

Eugene Cernan took this shot of the *Gemini 9* spacecraft while at the end of his umbilical tether during an early space walk. *(NASA, Thomas P. Stafford)*

activities and maneuvers were canceled because of excessive fuel consumption or faulty equipment. Two of the missions, *Gemini 6* and *9,* had to be rescheduled because the original liftoff rocket failed. Substitutions and replacements of crews because of illnesses, heart conditions, and the accidental death of two astronauts (Elliot See and Charles Bassett) during training meant a constantly changing schedule of assignments.

All of the astronauts pointed out that they had to be able to react to challenges when the missions did not quite go as predicted. So from the first, the astronauts argued that they were pilots, not just payloads and not just poster boys for NASA. The Original Seven and the New Nine were all qualified and trained as pilots, and all came to the space program from military careers.

APOLLO PROJECTS

The three-man Apollo projects began in 1967 and continued through 1971. After six unmanned flights of the equipment, the first manned shot, *Apollo 7*, was launched on October 11, 1968, to test the spacecraft in Earth's orbit. It had been delayed because of a tragic accident in January 1967, when three astronauts were killed in a fire in an Apollo capsule during a test on the ground. Gus Grissom, Edward White, and Roger Chaffee were testing the Apollo craft on the ground, wearing their space suits and breathing a pure oxygen atmosphere. The fire apparently started with some badly installed or defective wiring that was under one of the astronaut's couches. The door to the capsule was designed to open inward, and with the pressure from the burning plastic, Velcro, and other materials in the oxygen atmosphere, the astronauts could not open the door. It was several minutes before ground crews arrived to try to free the victims, and by then they had been asphyxiated by the poisonous gases released during the intense fire. This ground test, AS204–Block 1 (*Apollo-Saturn 204*, sometimes reported as *Apollo 1*), became the subject of much controversy.

Critics of the agency blamed NASA for not heeding warnings about the dangers of a pure oxygen atmosphere, especially in equipment test situations. The failure of the door, the slow response of rescue teams, the lack of firefighting equipment, and the decision by NASA to investigate its own accident, all caused negative reactions. Nevertheless,

Left to right: James Lovell, William Anders, and Frank Borman, the crew of *Apollo 8,* posed in front of a flight simulator. The crew orbited the Moon 10 times, as low as 70 miles above the surface, and then returned safely to the planned Pacific Ocean splashdown two days after Christmas 1968. *(NASA)*

MANNED APOLLO MISSIONS

Mission	Date	Astronauts	Objective(s)
AS204–Block 1	Jan. 27, 1967	Gus Grissom, Edward White, and Roger Chaffee	ground test; three die in fire
Apollo 7	Oct. 11, 1968	Wally Schirra, Donn Eisele, and Walter Cunningham	Earth orbit
Apollo 8	Dec. 21, 1968	Frank Borman, Jim Lovell, and William Anders	lunar orbit
Apollo 9	March 3, 1969	James McDivitt, David Scott, and Russell Schweikart	Earth orbit
Apollo 10	May 18, 1969	Thomas Stafford, John Young, and Gene Cernan	lunar orbit; "dress rehearsal"
Apollo 11	July 16, 1969	Neil Armstrong, Michael Collins, and Edwin Aldrin	first Moon landing
Apollo 12	Nov. 14, 1969	Charles Conrad, Richard Gordon, and Alan Bean	second Moon landing
Apollo 13	April 11, 1970	Jim Lovell, Fred Haise, and John Swigert	service module accident
Apollo 14	Jan. 31, 1971	Alan Shepard, Stuart Roosa, and Edgar Mitchell	third Moon landing
Apollo 15	July 26, 1971	David Scott, Alfred Worden, and James Irwin	fourth Moon landing; use Lunar Rover Vehicle
Apollo 16	April 16, 1972	John Young, Thomas Mattingly II, and Charles Duke	fifth Moon landing
Apollo 17	Dec. 7, 1972	Gene Cernan, Ronald Evans, and Harrison Schmitt	sixth and final Moon landing
Apollo 18–20			canceled

the agency had such a reservoir of goodwill that the media generally remained supportive. The tragic deaths were mourned, and the program went ahead, struggling to meet the deadline of a man on the Moon by the end of the 1960s.

APOLLO 11:
A Dream Fulfilled

The most memorable and dramatic of the flights was the first to land on the Moon, *Apollo 11*, in July 1969. The trip not only represented the fulfillment of President Kennedy's challenge, made in 1961, but captured the imagination of the world. In many ways, *Apollo 11* was the culmination of long-standing human aspirations to travel from Earth and land on another world.

The three-part spacecraft, consisting of a lunar module (LM), command module, and service module, would speed from Earth's orbit to the Moon's orbit. There, the LM would separate from the joined command and service modules. One astronaut would remain aboard the command module, while the other two descended in the LM to get out and walk on the surface of the Moon. Altogether there were six successful lunar landings.

The world watched *Apollo 11* intently, as the two astronauts experimented with walking in the reduced lunar gravity. Armstrong noted that the surface was "fine and powdery" and that he could pick it up loosely with the toe of his boot. Aldrin remarked at the view: "magnificent desolation." The shots of their footprints in the dust of the Moon and their attempts to develop kangaroo hops were avidly watched everywhere on Earth where there were television receivers. Armstrong and Aldrin gathered some samples of rock, and after nearly a day on the surface, they lifted off the surface for a safe mating with the command module and a return to a heroes' welcome on Earth. But NASA found that the public's fascination with the Apollo missions and with the Moon soon waned.

The fire on *AS204* and the near-disaster of the *Apollo 13* mission did not deter the completion of the remaining missions. However, many of the astronauts waiting their turn for a chance to continue Moon exploration were disappointed when NASA decided to cancel Moon-landing missions *Apollo 18, 19,* and *20.*

NASA canceled the last trips partly because public interest had declined, despite the six successful returns of astronauts from the Moon with collections of gathered mineral samples. One aspect of having set such a specific goal in 1961 was that it later became difficult to justify continuing the mission for solely scientific results. As outlined by Vice President Johnson in early 1961, the mission had been quite clear: Beat the Soviet Union to the Moon. Once that goal had been achieved, the always-secondary scientific side no longer seemed worth the expenditure of billions of dollars.

The boot prints of the astronauts may remain on the surface of the Moon for centuries, silent testimony to the human spirit of exploration. *(NASA)*

One Small Step

On July 20, 1969, knowing that a major historical event was about to take place, astronaut Neil Armstrong prepared himself with a memorable line. Yet stepping down out of the lunar lander took considerable preparation. Six hours and 21 minutes after landing, Armstrong and Edwin "Buzz" Aldrin pulled open the hatch, and Aldrin watched as Armstrong slowly backed out of the lander, moving his bulky backpack carefully side to side. Armstrong then lowered himself to one of the landing pads that were like feet on the lander.

He checked to make sure he could step back up from the landing pad to the first rung on the ladder, then he stepped off onto the surface. A television camera aboard the ship transmitted his image as he said, "That's one small step for man, one giant leap for mankind."

Later, observers debated whether he had meant ". . . one small step for *a* man . . ." Armstrong thought he had said it that way, but when he listened to the tape, he could not tell whether the broadcast failed to pick up his word, or whether, in the excitement, he had dropped the word *a*. With or without the *a*, it really was a giant leap for mankind.

Soon Aldrin came out and together the two astronauts planted a plaque that read: "Here Man from the planet Earth first set foot upon the Moon, July 1969 A.D. We came in peace for all mankind." Aldrin and Armstrong then raised an American flag, on a pole that did not quite stick properly in the hard surface.

Michael Collins, circling in the command module above the surface of the Moon, heard from flight control that the flag had been set. He noted dryly that he was probably the only person in the universe who was not watching the event on television.

Opposite page: Neil Armstrong took this picture of Edwin "Buzz" Aldrin during the first walk on the Moon on the *Apollo 11* mission in 1969. Reflected in Aldrin's face shield are the leg of the lunar module and Armstrong himself. *(NASA)*

THE MOON IN THIS DECADE:
Assessment

The accomplishment of the Moon mission achieved its intended propaganda purpose. While part of the apparent 1961 lead of the Soviets had been manufactured by Soviet premier Khrushchev's manipulation of informa-

tion, popular opinion nevertheless held in the early 1960s that the United States was "behind." That impression was gone by the end of 1969.

Beyond the propaganda and self-image question, there were other consequences of the Moon race. The success of Project Apollo gave a boost to the concept that problems could be addressed by a concerted national effort. Over the 20 years following the landing

on the Moon, when Americans tackled challenging domestic issues and searched for solutions, reference to this national achievement often served as a point of comparison or a rallying point: "If we can land a man on the Moon, why can't we . . .?" [finishing with such ideas as "end poverty," "find a cure for cancer," or "clean up the environment"]. Of course, many problems were not as easily addressed by technology and money as the problem of reaching the Moon; nevertheless, the can-do attitude embodied in Kennedy's challenge and in NASA's response did suggest that marshaling a national effort behind a specific goal was possible in the United States.

An important by-product of the Moon race was the Outer Space Treaty signed in 1967. Henceforth, the arms incentive for space exploration would be reduced, and the focus could truly rest on scientific exploration. Many saw the Moon trip as a great step in the long adventure of humankind's exploration. It did mark the beginning of humans' venturing into space. In the next decades, that exploration focused less on the spectacular competitive achievement of manned space travel to other worlds and more on a step-by-step gathering of information by a wide variety of means.

The landing of *Apollo 11* on July 18, 1969, was viewed by many as the beginning of the space age. Outer space may have been already conquered with astronauts in orbit and on the surface of the Moon, but the mysteries of the

This picture of the Earth, taken by the *Apollo 8* astronauts, showed it as a blue marble rising over the surface of the Moon. The image became an icon for a "whole-earth" perspective in the 1970s. *(NASA)*

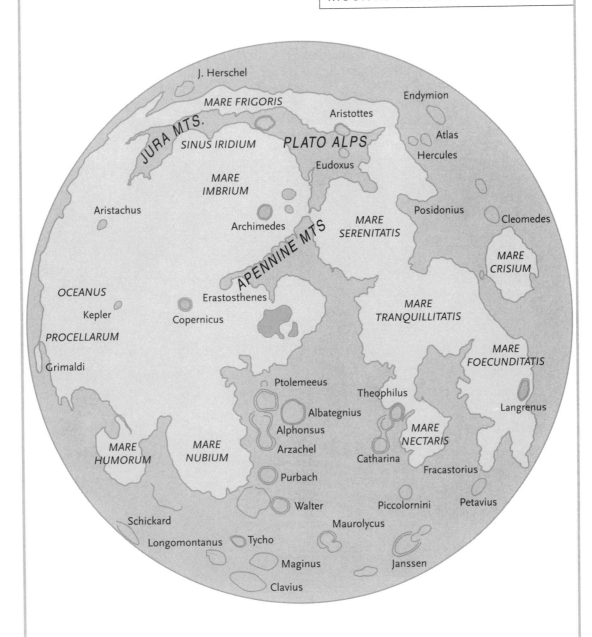

J. Herschel

MARE FRIGORIS

Endymion

Aristottes

JURA MTS.

SINUS IRIDIUM

PLATO ALPS

Atlas

Hercules

Eudoxus

MARE IMBRIUM

Aristachus

Posidonius

Cleomedes

Archimedes

MARE SERENITATIS

APENNINE MTS

MARE CRISIUM

OCEANUS

Kepler

Erastosthenes

Copernicus

MARE TRANQUILLITATIS

PROCELLARUM

Grimaldi

MARE FOECUNDITATIS

Ptolemeeus

Theophilus

Langrenus

Albategnius

Alphonsus

MARE NECTARIS

Arzachel

Catharina

MARE HUMORUM

MARE NUBIUM

Purbach

Fracastorius

Walter

Piccolornini

Petavius

Schickard

Maurolycus

Longomontanus

Tycho

Janssen

Maginus

Clavius

PLATO ALPS Mountain ranges
MARE NECTARIS Mares or plains
Tycho Craters

Astronauts Dave Scott and Jim Irwin of the *Apollo 15* crew explored the surface of the Moon in 1971 in this lunar rover, that had a top speed of about seven miles an hour. *(NASA, James B. Irwin)*

universe continued to lure the human race on to further exploration.

Even as the race for the Moon was in progress, planners and engineers in the Soviet Union and the United States anticipated the next steps in the exploration of space. Orbiting space stations, robotic trips to other planets, and improved observation from Earth could combine to further push back the frontier.

6

SPACE STATIONS

Dreamers and enthusiasts such as Wernher von Braun and Robert Goddard had visualized the day when rockets would carry humans into outer space. They and hundreds of science fiction authors writing in the 1940s and 1950s believed that by the end of the 20th century, human beings would have permanent settlements off planet Earth. Their expectations turned out to be almost right. The United States put *Skylab* in orbit in 1973; on this space station small groups of astronauts could be in space for periods of more than 100 days each, during which several shifts of crews gathered valuable information. In 1986, the Soviets placed *Mir* in orbit, sending up a total of five modules that were linked together into a true space station. After 15 years of service and several near-disasters, the *Mir* was brought down in a fiery descent into the Pacific Ocean in 2001. More ambitious and more permanent was the *International Space Station*, assembled over a period of seven years, 1998–2004, and supported by more than a dozen nations. By the early 21st century, there was indeed a near-permanent presence of the human race living off the planet Earth.

SKYLAB

Skylab was launched May 14, 1973, with the objective of learning exactly how humans could live in space for an extended period of time. The *Gemini 7* crew of Frank Borman and James Lovell had stayed in space for almost two weeks, and a Russian team aboard *Soyuz 9* were in orbit for 18 days, but medical specialists worried that longer exposures to weightlessness might have permanent damaging physical effects. Scientists also wondered about the psychological effects of weightlessness and confinement in space, and a lengthy stay would provide an opportunity to study those questions in addition to the physical effects.

Furthermore, a longer stay might allow some experiments in working with materials in a gravity-free environment, opening the possibility of future manufacturing processes in space. As plans matured for *Skylab*, other missions were tacked on, including observations of Earth, experiments in space physics, and in biology. As the design of *Skylab* evolved, many new concepts emerged, such as floors and ceilings made of open gridwork.

Problems of waste disposal, bathing, communication, sleeping and eating accommodations, and a gravity-free work environment all had to be dealt with.

The original idea for *Skylab* was to orbit an empty rocket fuel tank that would then be equipped with facilities for living, communication, and a workshop-laboratory. However, as

Astronaut Charles Conrad, Jr., trains for the first mission aboard *Skylab*, working with space manufacturing equipment in a simulation facility at the Johnson Space Center. *(NASA)*

plans developed and the difficulty of construction in space was better understood, NASA decided to equip *Skylab* on the ground and send it into space ready to receive humans.

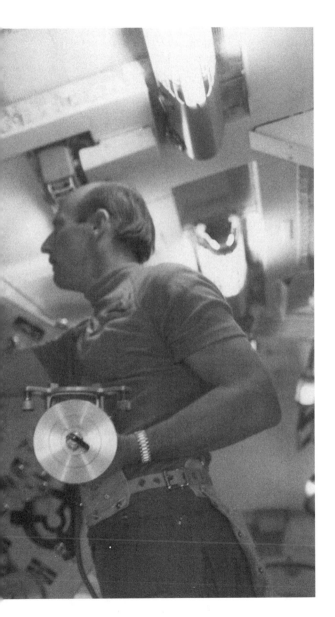

Skylab had outside dimensions about 48 feet by about 22 feet, with an internal space to live and work in about 1,100 cubic feet. This meant that a crew of three would live, work, eat, sleep, and use the bathroom in an area about the size of a small to medium-sized camping trailer. Power was provided by solar arrays arranged on deployed wings. Since the *Skylab* would orbit out of the sunlight about one-third of the time, a system of batteries stored power gathered by the solar arrays while they were in the sunlit period of the orbit. Rotating the laboratory through the sunlight and into shade provided heating and cooling. Prior to the arrival of each crew, the atmosphere inside the craft would be circulated and purified.

Altogether, three separate manned missions were scheduled, totaling 171 days in space over a period of nine months. Before *Skylab* was launched, it was not known what effect prolonged exposure to space radiation would have on the crew or on materials, sensors, and electrical components aboard the craft. Careful measurements taken before the first crew was sent up, showed that exposure was within safe limits.

Although the planning called for *Skylab* to be maintenance-free, it became clear that the crews would have to conduct numerous repairs as unexpected problems developed. The crews learned every detail of the *Skylab* mechanical systems and familiarized themselves with the tools, spares, filters, waste equipment, and assorted backup hardware. Special procedures were worked out for more than 150 different repair tasks and the crew practiced all of them. A general-purpose tool kit included tape, wire, pliers, string, tweezers, and other handy items that might prove essential. The first mission involved lots of repair work to *Skylab,* which was damaged on takeoff.

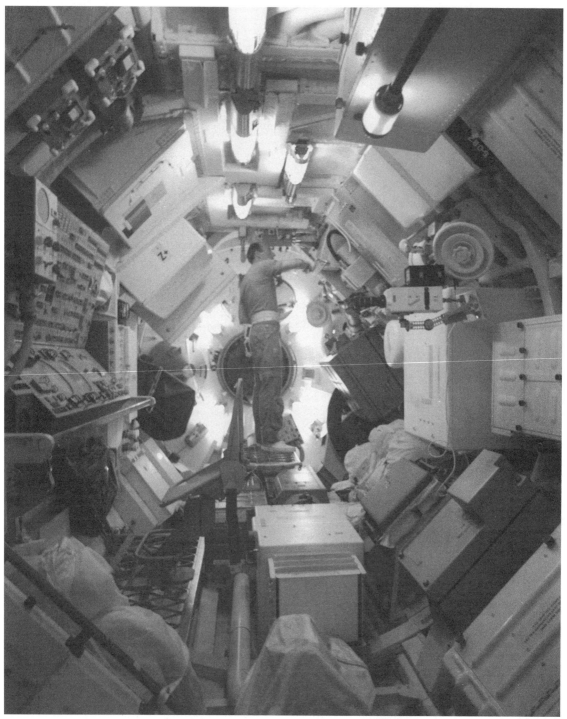

Ground training in the simulator for *Skylab* involved learning the placement of dozens of experiments in the cramped quarters. *(NASA)*

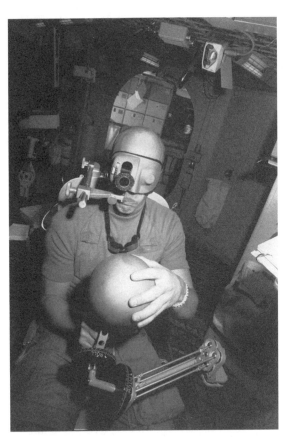

Among many experiments planned for *Skylab* were tests of the ability of astronauts to maintain their sense of orientation in the weightless environment. In this ground-based orbital workshop, astronaut Charles Conrad, Jr., practices in a rotating and tilting chair while blindfolded. *(NASA)*

Each of the three crews had a backup crew, and many of the astronauts training for the *Skylab* missions had never been in space before. However, Charles Conrad, who had flown on *Gemini 5* and *Gemini 11* and had walked on the Moon on *Apollo 12*, headed the first crew. Alan Bean, who had been the lunar module pilot on *Apollo 12*, headed the second team. The three manned missions provided vast quantities of data on the problems of liv-

ing in a weightless environment and began to lay the groundwork for longer stays in space aboard future space stations.

MIR

Space exploration programs in the Soviet Union also included plans for regularly lifting crews from Earth and taking them to orbiting satellites, where they could conduct observations, build their own living and working spaces, and begin programs of regular scientific work. The Soviets used their large rockets to launch Salyut capsules, containing astronauts and equipment.

In 1986, the Soviets built a more permanent space station, known as *Mir*, that remained in operation for 15 years. The first *Mir* crew, Leonid Kizim and Vladimir Soloviev, opened the station and then ferried aboard a Soyuz spacecraft to *Salyut 7*, which was still in orbit, where they spent almost two months. In March 1987, a second module, known as *Kvant 1*, arrived at the *Mir* station to be docked; however, a problem developed, when the hatches between the two modules could not be opened. Members of the crew, in an unscheduled space walk, found that a prior visit by a Progress cargo ship had left a bag of trash that jammed the hatch opening. Two cosmonauts installed new solar panels on the core module of *Mir*. Beginning in 1987, crews regularly rotated for long stays aboard *Mir*. The regular rotations continued for two years, when they were interrupted because a relief crew could not arrive in time to replace a departing crew.

Numerous astronauts from other nations visited *Mir* for short stays, including French air force pilot Jean-Loup Chrétien and crewmembers from Syria and Afghanistan. Later, Toyohiro Akiyama, as a Japanese "space correspondent," visited the *Mir* station and conducted a live broadcast for a Tokyo television station. In 1989, the *Kvant 2* module was attached. In 1990, working with a tethered line, cosmonauts Alexander Serebrov and Alexander Victorenko rode in "flying armchairs" more than 100 feet from the station.

Simply supplying and occupying the station required several on-the-job adjustments and temporary fixes, reflecting the ingenuity of the Russian teams. During a space walk in 1990, cosmonauts repaired a thermal layer on the Soyuz spacecraft that was used to shuttle crews up to the *Mir* and back to Earth. They had never been specifically trained to make

the repair, which they pulled off successfully. However, as they returned to *Mir*, they damaged an airlock and had to go back into *Mir* by way of a compartment in the *Kvant 2* module.

After the dissolution of the Soviet Union in 1991, *Mir* received crews that included astronauts from Austria and from the former Soviet republic of Kazakhstan, with later visits in 1992 by astronauts from Germany and France. Several records were set by the crews aboard *Mir*, including the longest stay in space by Valeri Polyakov, who returned in 1995 from a 438-day stay aboard. The U.S. space shuttle *Atlantis* docked with *Mir* in 1995, and Norman

Salyut Stations

The Soviet Union launched the space station *Salyut 6* in September 1977. The five prior Salyut stations had either failed or stayed in orbit briefly. On one, *Salyut 4*, launched in 1974, the system to remove moisture condensing from the cosmonaut's breath failed, leading to fogged-up windows and green mold on the walls. By contrast *Salyut 6* was fairly successful. After some problems with docking, two cosmonauts, Yuri Romanenko and Georgi Grechko, settled in to *Salyut 6* for a lengthy stay. The Salyut was equipped with exercise equipment, including a treadmill, a stationary bike, and bungee cords. Unfortunately, there was no way to take a bath aboard the craft, and the cosmonauts did not like the way they smelled after exercising. During the stay, they were visited by two other cosmonauts aboard a Soyuz rocket, and they received a supply of food, mail, and some clean clothes from a Progress supply ship. Romanenko and Grechko loaded the empty supply rocket with garbage and sent it back to burn up in the atmosphere. On another visit by a Soyuz, they received a visit from a Czech cosmonaut, the first person in space who was neither Soviet nor American.

Romanenko and Grechko came back to Earth in March 1978, after a total of 96 days in orbit, the record up to that time. From this and other long stays in space, doctors learned that weightlessness led to a loss of bone mass from the hips and spine.

The Soviet Union followed up with *Salyut 7*, launched in 1982. Over the period between 1977 and 1985, the two successful Salyut stations had a total of 10 long-duration stays by cosmonauts, and the stations were occupied for nearly half the time over the eight-year period.

Thagard, an American astronaut, conducted experiments on the Russian station for several months. Several other Americans spent vari- ous periods up to a few months over the next two years aboard the *Mir*. In 1996, an Ameri- can woman astronaut, Shannon Lucid, spent

Traveling aboard a Soyuz supply vessel, Russian cosmonauts caught this picture of the space shuttle *Atlantis* departing from the *Mir* space station. The five linked modules of the *Mir* remained in space for 15 years. *(NASA)*

During her long stay aboard the *Mir*, Shannon Lucid keeps up her exercises using a treadmill in the base block module of the Russian space station. *(NASA)*

almost six months aboard, setting a record for the longest stay by an American astronaut in space up to that time.

In 1997, the station suffered some of its worst accidents up to that time. In February, a lithium candle, which when burned gave off oxygen, got out of hand and started a fire aboard *Mir*. It took the crew more than an hour to extinguish the fire. Flames behave very differently in a weightless environment, and the fire could easily have killed the whole crew aboard and destroyed the station. Later, in June 1997, a Progress cargo craft veered off course and banged into the station a number of times, puncturing one of the modules, which started to lose pressure. Working

quickly, the crew, including one American, managed to cut cables that led through a hatch door to the punctured compartment and sealed it off before the pressure inside the main part of the *Mir* station fell too low. After several more international visits to the now damaged and increasingly dirty station, the last crew left *Mir* in 1999.

An American businessman began a program to train astronauts to repair *Mir* and to put visits to it on a commercial basis, and the first repair team went up in April 2000. However, that plan and others to turn the station to a profit all fell through, and the Russian space agency decided that the safest course of action would be to bring *Mir* down. The "deor-

Shuttle-*Mir* Program

Over a 27-month period from 1996 to 1998, a team of American astronauts lived and worked aboard the *Mir* space station for various periods. The program was in preparation for the assembly and operation of the *International Space Station*. The objectives of the Shuttle-*Mir* Program were to gain experience in Russian-American cooperation and practices, to reduce the construction costs and risks for the *International Space Station* by testing out various designs and procedures, to gain experience on missions of long duration, and to conduct some research, especially under conditions of microgravity. Among the discoveries was that living in microgravity causes a 1.2 percent loss of bone mass in the lower hip and spine per month. Other experiments showed that plants could be grown and the seeds could be harvested, proving that it would be possible to set up a greenhouse in outer space for extended life sustenance.

Space shuttle *Atlantis*, its cargo bay open, orbits directly below the *Mir* space station during one of many visits. *(NASA)*

biting" was a bit risky because *Mir* was the largest human-made object ever to be aimed down at Earth from outer space, weighing 135 tons. The earlier descent of space station *Salyut 7* in 1991 after it had been vacated and then fired down through the atmosphere had a planned landing in the Pacific Ocean. The 40-ton *Salyut 7* went off course and crashed into South America, fortunately in an unpopulated region. The much larger and heavier *Mir*, with its five separate linked modules, was predicted to break apart. When the Progress rockets fired, it forced the *Mir* into the proper "footprint" of the Pacific. Observers on the Fiji Islands were treated to a spectacular fireworks display as the pieces of the station turned incandescent as they melted from the atmosphere's friction.

Although the *Mir* station was not equipped for much scientific work, it did provide a laboratory where the effects of living and working in space could be studied, and where cosmonauts and astronauts could learn how to cooperate in making EVAs, or space walks. Altogether, astronauts and cosmonauts from 10 different countries spent time gathering great amounts of data about the effects of weightlessness life in space.

INTERNATIONAL SPACE STATION (ISS)

The first parts of the *International Space Station (ISS)* were lifted into space in 1998, and construction proceeded in a step-by-step process into 2004. By the time of full deployment in 2004, it was to be capable of housing a permanent population of up to seven people. For visionaries of future exploration, the *ISS* would be humankind's first permanent off-Earth living facility, the first settlement of many that would continue to expand in future generations.

As in the past, skeptics criticized the vision, and funding of such efforts remained a difficult issue. Would there ever be payoffs, in any practical sense, other than the gaining of more knowledge? Similar doubts had troubled such great cross-ocean navigators as Columbus and Magellan, the mountain men, and the polar explorers. Would these outer space explorations represent the opening of new routes for trade, fortune, and economic benefit as those of Marco Polo and the conquistadores, or would the station simply represent an expensive set of tools for gaining scientific information? Planners hoped to address this concern by reiterating the many kinds of practical knowledge gained and the possibilities for commercial uses of the station and its laboratory and workshop.

Although the United States played a key role in launching and managing the *ISS* project, a group of 15 nations participated in the construction and launch of parts of the station and in providing crews. In addition to parts constructed by the United States and Russia, major components were provided by Canada, Brazil, Japan, and 10 member countries of the European Space Agency (ESA): Belgium, Denmark, France, Germany, Italy, the Netherlands, Norway, Spain, Sweden, and Switzerland. Both the Americans and the Russians drew on their prior experiences, with *Skylab* and with *Mir*, to plan and assemble the *ISS*.

BUILDING IN SPACE

The cooperation between Russia and the United States was extensive. The Russians launched their components and crews, sometimes including Americans or of other nationalities, from the Baikonur Cosmodrome near Tyuratum, Kazakhstan. The Americans supplied the station with components delivered by space shuttles launched from Cape

Astronauts John Herrington and Michael Lopez-Alegria kept from drifting away by short tether lines, work on the construction of the *International Space Station* during a scheduled EVA, or spacewalk. *(NASA)*

Canaveral, in Florida. The Russians put the first module in space. Known as *Zarya* (sunrise), it was launched in November 1998. The *Unity* module soon followed in the same month, taken on U.S. shuttle voyage STS-88.

Regular flights by both nations brought up supplies and cargo through 1999 and 2000. The Russians attached the *Zvezda* (star) service module in July 2000. Shuttle missions by *Discovery* and *Atlantis* took up supplies, batteries, and equipment for the living compartments. After installation of gyroscopes, crews began living aboard in November 2000. A laboratory developed in the United States was attached in January 2001, and crews were exchanged the following month. The Canada Arm, a long boom that allowed spacewalking astronauts to have a stable platform while attaching new parts and conducting maintenance outside the station was added in 2001, together with a special airlock that was designed to accommodate both the Russian-style and American-style space suits. Italy and Japan provided other modules.

When completed, the *ISS* would have a 365-foot wingspan and a total mass of 1 mil-

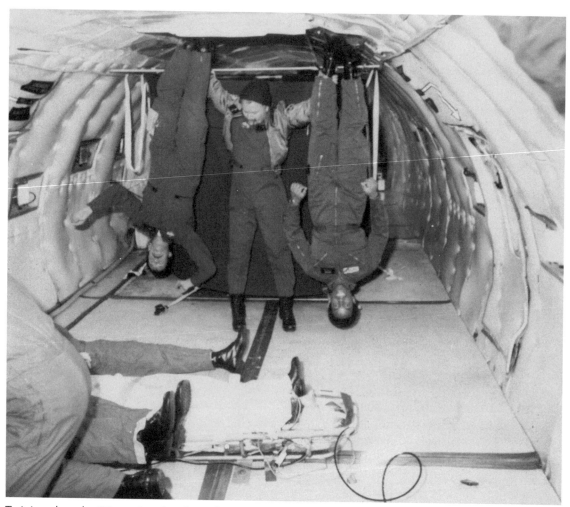

Training aboard a KC-135 aircraft, informally known as the "vomit comet," Guion Bluford *(right)*, Charles Hayes *(left)*, and C. P. Stanley *(center)* briefly experience weightlessness as part of astronaut training. *(NASA)*

lion pounds, or three times that of the huge *Mir* station that had been assembled in the 1980s and 1990s. The *ISS* is to accommodate a crew up to seven and will contain six separate laboratories. Rotating some 220 miles above Earth, its completion will require more than 1,000 hours of EVA, far more than the total of all other prior missions in space.

INTERNATIONAL EFFORT

Although cooperation in space between the Soviet Union and the United States had begun in the 1970s, the *International Space Station* represented a concerted effort to make this endeavor truly international. In addition to the Russian-American cooperation, many other countries participated with crucial parts of the final station. Canada provided the Space Station Remote Manipulator System, which was an improvement over the original mechanical arm designed and built in Canada. Canada also developed the robotic Canada Hand, or Special Purpose Dexterous Manipulator.

The ESA (a consortium of 11 countries) built a pressurized laboratory, launched on a French rocket. Japan provided an exterior platform for experiments and also logistics transport vehicles. Russia provided two research modules as well as the station's living quarters. In addition, the Russians built the science power platform of solar arrays and regularly supplied the *ISS* with their transport vehicles launched from Baikonur. Other pieces of equipment from Brazil and Italy included a pallet to house external payloads, unpressurized logistics carriers, and an Earth observation facility.

The object of the *ISS* was not simply to demonstrate that international cooperation was possible or that humans could live and work for extended periods in space. Rather, the nations cooperated to build a permanent laboratory in space that could be used to host a wide variety of practical experiments. Researchers planned protein crystal studies and examinations of tissue culture. They sought to learn how life in low gravity would affect humans, plants, insects, and other life forms. They would study the characteristics of flames, fluids, and molten metal in space, in the emerging new fields of combustion science and materials science. Others planned experiments in fundamental physics and the nature of space. The station would provide an ideal platform for observation of Earth. Furthermore, the station opened up possible commercialization ventures, with small-scale work on manufacturing processes to determine what new types of pharmaceuticals and microscopic technologies (known as nanotechnology) might be best made in a gravity-free environment.

There was a darker backdrop to this harmonic international venture, however. As the *International Space Station* was being constructed, critics on Earth pointed to the tragedies that had accompanied space travel, including the failure of two of America's shuttle craft with the complete loss of life of their crews.

7

THE SPACE SHUTTLES

As the American public turned their attention away from Project Apollo, NASA tried to demonstrate the practical results that could be derived from space exploration. The early efforts with *Skylab* showed that budgets and support could be mustered for an ongoing research program in outer space. Thus, the concept of reusable, rather than expendable crafts, support vehicles, and launchers developed, resulting in the space shuttle program.

THE SHUTTLE FLEET

The space shuttle, also known as an orbiter vehicle (OV), represented a compromise system that was controversial from its beginnings. Not a true space airplane, the shuttle would contain a crew compartment and a cargo space about the size of a large school bus that would be lifted into space on expendable Saturn rockets. The shuttle would orbit for one or two weeks to allow crews to conduct experiments, place or retrieve satellites or repair them, launch interplanetary automated space exploration craft, and perform other jobs. The shuttle would then return to Earth,

not as a powered aircraft, but as a glider, simply aiming down through the atmosphere with minor corrections to its angle of descent, to land at specified large runways. With engines installed but not loaded with fuel, the shuttles weighed more than 170,000 pounds. Each was designed to accommodate a seven-member crew.

To transport a shuttle from one location to another, it would be placed piggyback on a Boeing 747 jet aircraft and carried as cargo to facilities for repair and refurbishment. Although writers often referred to *the space shuttle*, altogether there were six shuttles built in the 20th century. The first, named *Enterprise* after the science fiction spacecraft in Eugene Roddenberry's television show, *Star Trek*, was designated OV-101, even though it never went into orbit. Instead, *Enterprise* was built to test the difficult glider landing, habitability, instrumentation, and the unique system of heat-resistant ceramic tiles that coated the craft.

The other five craft were named after great ships that had once been engaged in exploration by sea: the *Columbia*, built in 1981; the *Challenger*, built in 1982; the *Dis-*

Space shuttle *Columbia,* one of five orbiter vehicles to have been launched into space, lifts off on the first shuttle mission in 1981. *(NASA)*

THE SHUTTLE FLEET

Enterprise OV-101	test vehicle only, never launched into space; retired to Smithsonian Institution in 1985
Columbia OV-102	flew 27 missions, 1981–2003; broke up on 28th mission, February 1, 2003
Challenger OV-99	flew 9 missions, 1982–86; exploded 59 seconds into launch on 10th mission, January 28, 1986
Discovery OV-103	flew 30 missions, 1983–2003
Atlantis OV-104	flew 26 missions, 1984–2003
Endeavour OV-105	replaced *Challenger;* flew 19 missions, 1992–2003

covery, built in 1983; the *Atlantis,* in 1984; and the *Endeavour,* built in 1992 to replace the *Challenger.* Both *Columbia* and *Challenger* were lost in tragic accidents, representing 40 percent of the orbit-capable shuttle fleet. Those losses raised serious questions about the management of the shuttle program and of NASA itself. The questions went to the heart of whether manned space travel was a wise idea.

THE MISSIONS

The 111 successful missions of the space shuttle program have included a wide range of activities. At first NASA planners had hoped that the shuttles could be used to provide a practical, reliable, and routine trucklike service to outer space. Customers could be charged for services rendered, such as placing a satellite in orbit or recovering one that was malfunctioning or had not reached its proper altitude. Several of the early missions in the period 1981–85 by *Columbia* and *Challenger* were just such jobs. In order to attract business, NASA would charge $42 million for a flight to space, even though the estimated

cost of one such mission ran about $140 million. In this fashion, NASA hoped to undercut operations by the French commercial rocket service and to make its services attractive to the U.S. military. However, after the *Challenger* disaster in January 1986, the shuttles were prohibited by law from carrying commercial cargoes. Even before that accident, the Defense Department announced that it would launch its expensive surveillance satellites by expendable rockets (with proven records of reliability) rather than on the shuttle. As a moneymaking business, the shuttles clearly were not competitive.

Other problems with the original plan to convert the shuttles into a regular "truck line to space" soon developed. The first concepts had called for the fleet to make as many as 50 visits to outer space every year. By the mid-1980s, planners had settled on a less ambitious but still heavy schedule of some 24 visits per year. Originally NASA had hoped that between each flight, a shuttle would need about 10 days for maintenance and minor repairs. However, as tiles were damaged and other equipment found faulty and in need of replacement, the average time for maintenance and refurbishment between flights of a single shuttle stretched to more than two months on average. With budget cutbacks, parts from one shuttle craft would be removed and used as replacements on another, a process known as cannibalization.

Even so, of the 111 space shuttle missions, some were important to space exploration and the placement and repair of the *Hubble Space Telescope* and other types of telescopes in orbit around the Earth. Among the crucial missions were visits to the *Mir* space station to exchange crews and conduct experiments about living and working in outer space, and the transport of pieces of the *International Space Station.*

Even before the *Challenger* accident in 1986, critics charged that the shuttle was based on a faulty idea, combining a partial aircraft (reduced to a return glider) with vertical liftoff rockets falling away as the shuttles lifted out of the atmosphere. The compromise design meant that astronauts aboard the shuttles had to face the risk of being strapped to highly explosive fuel for liftoff and face a highly risky descent without power. Furthermore, unlike an airliner, if the shuttle missed its landing field, it could not turn around for a

A shuttle is moved from the vehicle assembly building to its launch site by "crawler transporter." *(NASA)*

return. Most of the landings were conducted at Edwards Air Force base in California, and then the shuttle would be flown piggyback aboard a 747 jet back to Florida for its next mission.

CHALLENGER

Challenger's launch on its 10th mission, in January 1986, was controversial. Even though Florida is generally warm in the winter, during the three days preceding the January 28 liftoff, the local weather had dropped severely. At launch time, it was 36° Fahrenheit, some 15 degrees colder than the coldest prior launch. On previous flights in cold weather, the O-rings that joined the fuel tanks aboard the Saturn liftoff rockets had suffered serious erosion. These rubber rings sealed a flexible joint around the edges of the two fuel tanks, which were so large that they could not be transported by barge in single sections. When the O-rings hardened in the cold and lost their flexibility, the stresses from the expansion and contraction of the tanks due to differential temperatures caused minute cracks in the rings, which could allow leakage of the fuel. When engineers warned, before liftoff on January 28, 1986, that the cold air temperature could create a problem, management overruled their objections on the grounds that there was no proof that the temperature cre-

This picture of space shuttle *Challenger*, taken from a satellite orbiting above it, shows the cargo bay doors opened to the side and the manipulator arm partially extended. *(NASA)*

Naming the Shuttles

After selecting the name *Enterprise* for the experimental shuttle that would be used solely to test gliding, landing, and other performance aspects of the craft, NASA decided to name the rest of the fleet for famous sailing vessels.

Columbia was named for a sloop from Boston, Massachusetts, that was used in 1792 by Captain Robert Gray to explore the region around what is now southern British Columbia and the states of Washington and Oregon. Later, the first U.S. Navy ship to circumnavigate Earth also used the same name.

Challenger was named for the British Admiralty's research ship HMS *Challenger,* which was used to explore both the Atlantic and Pacific Oceans in the 1870s. The *Discovery* had originally been one of the two ships used in the 1770s by Captain James Cook in his explorations of the Pacific Ocean.

Atlantis was the name of a research ship owned by the Woods Hole Oceanographic Institute that operated out of its port in Massachusetts from 1930 to 1966. A two-masted ketch, it was the first American ship to be used exclusively for oceanographic work.

Endeavour was named after another of the exploring ships of Captain Cook. Cook sailed *Endeavour* in 1768 to the Pacific to observe the transit of Venus as it passed between the Earth and the Sun. With his measurements and calculations, the true distance of the Earth to the Sun (some 93 million miles) was calculated with accuracy.

---

ated increased risk. Furthermore, management argued, the schedule was important and should not be slipped because of presumed problems. Finally, the shuttles had operated in cold weather before and had experienced "normal" cracking of the O-rings.

On live television, as the rockets carrying *Challenger* lifted off, just 59 seconds into flight over the Atlantic, the rocket assembly suddenly exploded, showering debris and the crippled shuttle to the ocean. It took 22 seconds for *Challenger* to hit the ocean, when the crew was killed instantly. The nation and the world were stunned as the spectacular explosion replayed over and over on television.

As a result, all shuttle flights were grounded for 32 months, and an extensive investigation into the accident proceeded. Experts testified, as did the engineers who had protested against the flight. It was agreed that the O-rings and their exposure to intense cold indeed had been the immediate cause of the disaster; however, deeper causes were found, related to the corporate culture, or management style, of NASA itself.

Investigators for the official Rogers Commission pointed out that NASA had attempted to describe and treat the shuttle craft as an "operational" spacecraft, rather than an experimental craft, meaning that NASA had come to rely on the shuttle to perform regularly scheduled duties rather than continuing to test it and modify it. Furthermore, when small problems developed,

As *Challenger* lifted off, on January 28, 1986, a line of smoke leaking from the O-ring seal in the booster directly to the right of the *U* in United States was probably the first indication of the disaster to come less than a minute later. *(NASA)*

instead of regarding them as indicators of increased risk and a need for modification, management often chose to regard a successful flight with one of these identified problems as proof that the problem was an acceptable risk. As commission member Richard Feynman, who had won a Nobel Prize in physics in 1965, pointed out in his personal observations on the *Challenger* disaster, "NASA exaggerates the reliability of its product, to the point of fantasy."

Feynman compared NASA's expectation of acceptable performance of the shuttles with the damaged O-rings to a bridge designer expecting his bridge to carry heavy loads despite a large crack in the bridge after regular usage. If the bridge designer argued that the traffic proved that the bridge was able to carry the routine load with the crack, he would be acting irresponsibly. Instead, of course, the builder would note that the bridge had failed to meet its design specifications and would recommend barring traffic until full repairs with new materials could be achieved. NASA, however, had accepted the continued performance of its shuttles with flaws as evidence that the flaws did not matter.

The commission pointed out that NASA managers had become so used to thinking

The explosion of the *Challenger* was caught on video and immediately broadcast on television. *(NASA)*

Debris from the *Challenger* explosion over the ocean was collected and later entombed by being lowered into an abandoned missile silo at Cape Canaveral, Florida. *(NASA)*

The *Challenger* crew lost on January 28, 1986: (*Left to right, rear row*) Ellison Onizuka, Sharon Christa McAuliffe, Greg Jarvis, and Judy Resnik, (*left to right, front row*) Mike Smith, Francis Scobee, and Ron McNair. *(NASA)*

of the shuttles as routine and operational that the managers had decided it was even safe to send aloft politicians and others to gain public support. Senator Jake Garn of Utah, a supporter of NASA, flew aboard *Discovery* in April 1985; in January 1986, NASA sent up Congressman Bill Nelson of Florida on a *Columbia* mission. The crew on the last flight of *Challenger* had included a public school teacher, Christa McAuliffe, whom NASA had chosen from among 11,400 applicants.

Furthermore, observers noted, managers at NASA demanded that engineers prove the shuttle *unsafe* to fly before canceling a flight, rather than going by the rule that the shuttle should be proven safe to fly. Management's logic placed the burden of proof on engineers to interrupt a schedule, rather than placing the burden of proof on management to adhere to the schedule. Inside NASA, engineers had become used to deferring to management on policy and schedule decisions. All of these criticisms of the way that NASA managed the shuttle program were duly noted, and NASA undertook to alter its corporate culture.

COLUMBIA

On January 16, 2003, almost exactly 17 years to the day after the *Challenger* disaster, *Columbia* was launched on its 28th mission. Close observers and a few cameras noted that when the rockets lifted off their stand, large pieces of the foam covering the Saturn fuel tanks broke loose, and one of them appeared to strike the left wing of *Columbia*. In an intense round of e-mail correspondence and telephone conversations, engineers and managers discussed how important the foam breakage was. Managers pointed out that pieces of foam had broken loose many times before, and that the impacts had presented no hazard to the tiles on the wing. Often, the shuttles had returned with pockmarks or damaged tiles that would later be replaced during routine maintenance and refurbishment. The incident was routine, they argued. Some engineers, however, wanted to conduct tests to determine whether the foam had caused severe damage by setting up a test station while *Columbia* was in orbit. Management had the last say: Since the incident was routine, and there was no proof that the foam could cause a problem, no test would be funded.

The wreckage of *Columbia* was assembled from Texas and Louisiana for later study and analysis. *(NASA)*

On February 1, as the *Columbia* reentered the atmosphere after its two-week mission, observers on the ground, from California to Texas, could see the shuttle break up. Pieces were spread in a strip across Texas and into Louisiana, covering several hundred miles. There was no hope that any of the crew could have survived the impact. After the *Challenger* disaster, the shuttles had been equipped with parachutes that could be used, but only if the flight compartment stayed intact until a low enough altitude to deploy them. In this incident, the aluminum structure of the cabin could not withstand the force as the shuttle broke up.

A highly qualified Columbia Accident Investigation Board (CAIB) was convened to study the wreckage and to investigate the disaster. The official report concluded that the foam striking the left wing had indeed created damage to the wing. Recovered parts and pieces from the ground showed that metal parts inside the left wing had started to melt from the air friction, spreading droplets of molten metal that adhered to the tiles further back in the wing. From such evidence on tiles recovered on the ground and from close examination of some of the recorded instrument readings from the last few seconds of *Columbia*'s flight, it became clear that the foam had indeed broken or cracked the leading edge of the wing. A test was set up, shooting a piece of foam the size of the observed piece that broke from the fuel tanks against a mock-up of the leading edge of the wing. From the test, it was clear that foam, even though light, when traveling at several hundred miles an hour, could damage the leading edge tiles severely.

In addition to identifying the immediate causes of the accident, the CAIB once again criticized the NASA culture. The 2003 report was eerily similar to the report 17 years earlier, pointing to the same bad decision-making processes and management style.

A FLAWED CORPORATE CULTURE

The 2003 report concluded that both the *Challenger* and *Columbia* accidents derived from a failure of NASA's organizational system. Flying with known flaws had become routine and acceptable. When a design did not perform as expected, the deviation from expectation was reinterpreted as acceptable. As time passed and a flaw continued to be accepted, this practice led to diminishing perceptions of risk, and the culture defined problems as normal and routine. The report noted that, "If not corrected, the scene is set for another accident."

Other aspects of poor managerial style surfaced. NASA, in the interests of economy, had contracted out much of the work on parts, accepting contractors' own estimates of the quality of their work rather than NASA judging the quality itself. Downsizing and personnel cutbacks cut into safety staff, who were sent the signal or message that efficiency and keeping to schedule were of higher priority than safety was. The agency seemed to have inappropriately carried the "can-do" attitude of the Apollo days into the shuttle program. The schedule, rather than research, began to drive the program.

After *Challenger,* 17 years of 87 successful missions without serious accident had led to a false sense of confidence. Rules and procedures had taken precedence over engineering advice in both cases. The hierarchical management structure was the reverse of what should prevail. In a research organization with expertise at the lower levels of the organization, it was essential that a democratic style of decision making be encouraged. Instead,

NASA worked in a top-down manner, creating a culture that had existed for more than 20 years and was very disturbing to the investigation board. Furthermore, NASA's claim of having a "safety culture" was simply myth that resulted in tragic consequences for the crew members and their families.

Disturbing parallels between the two accidents worried the CAIB investigators. O-rings and foam debris were what the experts called "ill-structured problems" that needed to be uncovered. Although the causes for the two accidents were very different, the fact that they both derived from continuing low-level problems that had been ignored or dismissed as routine showed a serious and fundamental flaw in how NASA treated such difficulties. Similar continuing problems with the design needed to be ruthlessly examined and corrected.

The public dismay and scathing criticism from investigators reflected long-standing criticisms both of NASA and of the shuttle in particular. At the beginning of the 21st century, it was clear that NASA would need to seriously reexamine its own management style and that space travel and exploration by manned crews, if they were to go forward in the next decades, would have to be structured in a different and more sophisticated fashion.

8

UNMANNED SPACE EXPLORATION

 Although it is natural to think of space explorers as the astronauts and cosmonauts who travel into space, some of the most important space exploration has been performed by unmanned spacecraft. Sending astronauts into space puts the lives of men and women at risk. For this and many other reasons, exploration by unmanned spacecraft is preferable to transporting astronauts into space.

Among these reasons is that scientific equipment to conduct the exploration does not require food, water, or air to accompany or sustain it. Scientific sensors and cameras can be packed into much smaller spaces than life support systems required for astronauts. Thus, a spacecraft complete with radiation-detecting equipment, cameras, computers, and radios for transmitting data and receiving instructions can weigh just a few hundred pounds, rather than the tons required to sustain human life in outer space. Less weight requires less expensive rockets and less fuel. So unmanned craft not only are less risky but can be smaller and cheaper. Many of them can be sent for the same cost of sending one risky human-staffed exploration.

In a series of missions that sent out interplanetary probes beginning in 1969, human knowledge about the solar system has been greatly expanded. Although some of the missions failed, many sent back photographs, measurements, and new details about the Moon, Mercury, Venus, Mars, Jupiter, Saturn, Neptune, and Uranus, together with surprising details about some of the largest moons in the solar system that rotate around the planets Jupiter and Saturn. The craft discovered new moons and took close-up photographs of asteroids and Saturn's rings.

UNMANNED TO THE MOON

While Project Apollo was under way in the mid-1960s, NASA attempted several unmanned flights to the Moon with numerous disappointing failures and some eventual successes. In a series named Ranger, from 1961 through 1965, the first five rockets failed for a variety of reasons. Even after a personnel shakeup at the Jet Propulsion Lab (JPL) that had designed the on-board equipment, *Ranger 6,* launched in January 1964, still had defects, crashing on the Moon without sending pictures.

Finally, in July 1964, *Ranger 7* was a flawless success, sending pictures as it sailed down to the Moon, smashing as planned into Mare Nubium. JPL had mastered the challenges of careful, dust-free lab work and thorough testing of every part. *Ranger 8* and *9* in 1965 were also successes. *Ranger 9* pictures of the Moon's surface went directly to broadcast television, watched by millions of viewers.

Another craft, Surveyor, was planned to make an automated soft-landing on the Moon. The Soviet Union achieved such a landing in January 1966 with *Luna 9,* which sent back televised pictures from the surface more than two years before American astronauts landed there. The American *Surveyor 1* through *Surveyor 7,* designed by Hughes Aircraft, subsequently made successful Moon soft-landings and sent pictures between June 1966 and the end of 1967. NASA got detailed previews that would be useful to the astronauts.

THE PLANET MISSIONS

The numerous American unmanned spacecraft to other planets began in earnest with

UNMANNED EXPLORATIONS

Craft	Year	Planets Visited
Mariner 1	1962	mission failed
Mariner 2	1962	Venus, temperature measurements
Mariner 3	1964	mission failed
Mariner 4	1964–65	Mars flyby
Mariner 5	1967	Venus flyby
Mariner 6	1969	Mars flyby
Mariner 7	1969	Mars flyby
Mariner 8	1971	mission failed
Mariner 9	1971–72	Mars orbit
Mariner 10	1973–75	Venus flyby, Mercury flyby
Pioneer 10	1972–2003	Jupiter
Pioneer 11	1973–95	Jupiter, Saturn
Viking 1	1975–82	Mars orbiter and lander
Viking 2	1975–80	Mars orbiter and lander
Voyager 1	1977–80	Jupiter, Saturn and its moon, Titan
Voyager 2	1977–89	Jupiter, Saturn, Uranus, Neptune
Galileo	1989–97	Venus, asteroids, Jupiter orbiter and probe
Spirit and *Opportunity*	2003–04	Mars rovers

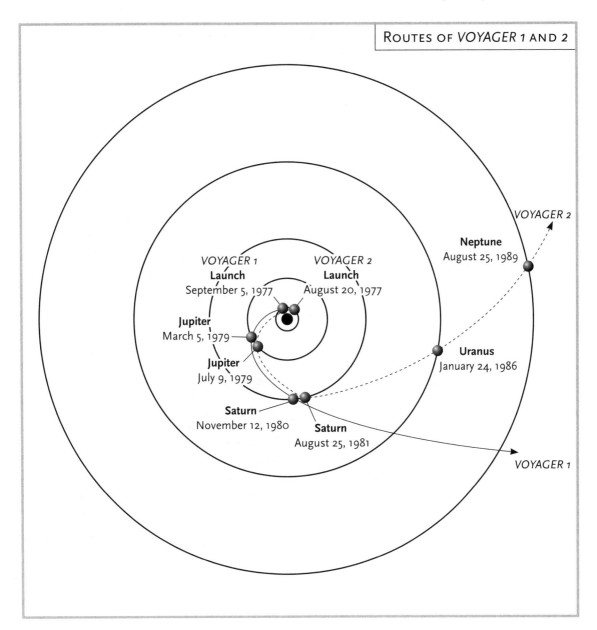

ROUTES OF *VOYAGER* 1 AND 2

VOYAGER 1
Launch
September 5, 1977

VOYAGER 2
Launch
August 20, 1977

Jupiter
March 5, 1979

Jupiter
July 9, 1979

Saturn
November 12, 1980

Saturn
August 25, 1981

Neptune
August 25, 1989

Uranus
January 24, 1986

VOYAGER 2

VOYAGER 1

eight Mariner flights between 1962 and 1975 that explored the planets Mars, Venus, and Mercury. Two missions dubbed Pioneer followed, using much the same equipment to explore out to the asteroid belt and Jupiter.

Most of these craft flew past their target planets, taking pictures as they went and relaying information back.

The Viking explorations of Mars over the period 1975–80 were more ambitious. The

The four largest moons of Jupiter *(in the bottom right corner)*, discovered by the astronomer Galileo Galilei in 1609, are known as the Galilean moons. They are shown here as photographed by *Voyager 1,* assembled in a collection: *(from back to foreground)* Io, then slightly down and to the left of Jupiter, Europa and Ganymede, with a section of Callisto showing in the lower right. *(NASA)*

Vikings orbited and relayed back information and included a lander that would descend to the surface of Mars and send back photographs and other information. A foremost objective of the Viking explorations was to determine if Mars had ever supported life. The accompanying table gives a chronology of the Mariner, Pioneer, and Viking interplanetary missions, as well as the unmanned Voyager and Galileo flights that followed.

One technique that helped in several of the later interplanetary voyages was using the gravity of one planet to pull in the spacecraft and then "slingshot" it on its way to the next destination. In 1965, an analyst at JPL, Gary Flandro, proposed the idea to speed up what would be a 30-year straight voyage out to Neptune. He pointed out that by using the planets' alignments properly, a single craft could be used to fly past Jupiter, Saturn, Uranus, and on to Neptune in as little as eight years. Studies showed that when *Mariner 4* had flown past Mars in 1964, it had picked up more than 3,000 feet per second in speed, the equivalent of a whole extra rocket stage. Using planets' gravity was like getting a free propulsion system.

By studying the expected alignments of the planets in 1977, and planning ahead from 1965 when Flandro suggested the idea, the scheme allowed for a tour of the planets utilizing this added gravity thrust. The idea was beautiful, but its cost limited the effort to *Voyager 1,* which would explore just Jupiter and Saturn, and *Voyager 2,* which would go on out to Neptune. To gain practice in the slingshot technique, JPL used the gravity of Venus to send *Mariner 10* toward Mercury in 1974.

That project worked fine. The added speed in orbit past Venus allowed *Mariner 10* to orbit around Mercury three times, taking and sending the closest, most accurate pictures of that planet's surface ever seen. Astronomers and the public were surprised to learn that the hot little planet nearest to the Sun was pockmarked with thousands of craters more clustered than those on the Moon. One crater in particular, named Caloris, was nearly one-third the diameter of the whole planet. Directly on the opposite side of Mercury, a jumbled region was a curious feature. NASA theorists suggested that it might have developed when a large impact of an asteroid on one side sent shock waves through the planet's surface to create the chaotic features on the opposite side. None of these details had ever been known before 1974, as they were simply too far away to be seen with the most powerful telescopes on Earth. Similarly, before *Voyager 1* was slingshot to Jupiter, astronomers had counted 13 moons of Jupiter; *Voyager 1* found another. To date, after other probes by later craft, at least 60 moons of the planet have been identified.

MARINER AND PIONEER

In carrying out the engineering work on the Mariner spacecraft, designers faced several challenges. The craft had to be provided with electrical energy in order to operate small motors to change camera angles and other sensors, to deploy antennas, to direct the angle of thruster propellants, and to turn on and off the thrusters. On-board computers and all the sensing equipment had to be warmed up to operate but could not be allowed to get too hot. Radio signals had to be received, despite any distortion and interference from magnetic fields in outer space, and they had to be properly interpreted. Data, including visual images, had to be sent back reliably to Earth.

Each of these issues required solutions that would weigh as little as was practical so that fuel would not be wasted. All of the unmanned spacecraft incorporated some ingenious designs to solve these problems. Some of the earliest computers did not perform as expected, and numerous mechanical problems plagued all the missions. Nevertheless, the gain in scientific knowledge was considerable.

The *Mariner 3* and *4* spacecraft were $9 \frac{1}{2}$ feet high by $22 \frac{1}{2}$ feet across. Into this space were packed a single camera that could take

21 pictures during a planetary flyby, together with a playback system that would take more than eight hours to send back a single picture. Other experiments included a measurement of Martian atmospheric pressure, a solar plasma probe, three Geiger counters for radiation measurement, a cosmic-ray telescope, and two cosmic-dust detectors. The position of the craft was determined by a sensor that would lock on the Sun and another that would detect the star Canopus. A small engine that could make two mid-course corrections was included. A computer and "mission sequencer" ensured each step in proper order. Power was provided by more than 28,000 solar cells and by batteries.

The *Mariner 6* and *7* craft each weighed 910 pounds, built on magnesium frames, 11 feet tall. Each carried four solar panels with a total of more than 83 square feet of exposed panels to pick up sunlight and convert it to electrical power. The intended missions for both craft were to fly past Mars and to take pictures. Each of these Mariners carried two cameras that were mounted on platforms that could be controlled from Earth to change angle and focus. Both craft sent back reams of data and hundreds of pictures that gave clear close-up images of the surface of Mars.

Although *Mariner 8* failed shortly after launch on May 8, 1971, *Mariner 9* combined all the mission objectives of the failed mission with its own. *Mariner 9* encountered the worst dust storm ever seen on Mars, but with control from Earth, the craft stayed in orbit, then began its mapping and its scientific measurements in late 1971 and early 1972.

Pioneer 10 and *11* were very different from the Mariners. They were built around a round 108-inch (9-foot) diameter antenna that unfolded like an umbrella. At the center of the antenna, a compact set of boxes contained experiments and equipment. Power came from two radioisotope thermoelectric generators (RTGs) mounted on booms that extended out from the equipment boxes. A third boom carried a magnetometer to measure magnetic fields. Many experiments and sensors packed inside included a meteorite detector, a plasma analyzer, a charged particle detector, a cos-

Radioisotope Thermoelectric Generator

A radioisotope thermoelectric generator, or radio-thermal generator (RTG), uses the heat derived from the decay of an isotope of plutonium to generate electricity. The first RTG was produced in 1958 using a concept developed by Thomas Seebeck (1770–1831) in the thermocouple. Seebeck's idea was to produce electrical current by keeping in contact two metals at different temperatures. In the RTG, the heat of radioactive decay heated a thermocouple that in turn produced electricity.

RTGs were used in the Pioneer, Viking, and Voyager space exploration vehicles. Because they contained a radioactive source that might interfere with instrument readings, the RTGs were located on long booms, remote from the sensing equipment.

NASA ARC   PIONEER 10   UNIV ARIZ
RANGE: 2965000 KM PHASE: 28.7   LCM2:   20
DATA RECEIVED 1 DEC 22:17:08 TO 1 DEC 22:37:46
A58 COLOR SECTOR 154 - 441 B 06/11/74

This closeup view of Jupiter taken from the *Pioneer 10* clearly shows the Great Red Spot, a permanent storm some 25,000 miles long, about three times the diameter of Earth. *(NASA)*

The *Viking 1* lander sent this picture back from the surface of Mars in 1976. *(NASA)*

mic-ray telescope, a Geiger tube telescope, and photometers to measure both infrared and ultraviolet light. The total weight of 570 pounds included 66 pounds of scientific instrumentation.

The missions of the *Pioneer 10* and *11* were to explore Jupiter and its nearby space, investigate the asteroid belt, and test conditions out as far as the orbit of Saturn, about 1 billion miles from the Sun. By sending back the details on radiation, asteroid and meteorite particles, and magnetic fields, these Pioneer crafts transmitted data that would be useful for later flights. *Pioneer 10* came within 81,000 miles of Jupiter in 1973. In 1987, *Pioneer 10* became the first human-made object to leave the whole solar system. *Pioneer 11* came within 27,000 miles of Jupiter and approached within 21,000 miles of Saturn's rings in 1979.

VIKING AND VOYAGER

The *Viking 1* and *2* spacecraft included two sections: One was designed to orbit Mars, while the other would make a soft-landing on the planet to gather information from the surface. The orbiter's communication system would be used to boost and relay the signals from the lander back to Earth. For this reason, the orbiter systems included powerful and delicate antennas designed both to pick up the signals from the surface and from Earth and to send messages back to Earth. When the *Viking 1* lander touched down on Mars on July 20, 1976, it was the first spacecraft built by the United States to do so. The Soviet Union had already landed a craft on Mars. *Viking 2*'s lander touched down on September 2, 1976, and continued to send data, including photographs, until April 1980.

The Voyagers undertook the most ambitious missions up to that time, the planet tours. The most prominent feature of the Voyager spacecraft was a large, 12-foot diameter antenna, always aimed back at Earth throughout the mission. A computer allowed storage of commands to control experiments and flight and to deploy equipment. Like the Vikings, the Voyagers were powered by RTGs. In addition to sensing and transmitting electromagnetic data, both Voyagers transmitted spectacular pictures of Jupiter and its moons back to Earth. *Voyager 1* took pictures of Sat-

urn's moon Titan, then headed out of the solar system, while *Voyager 2* continued to take and transmit back pictures of the outer planets Uranus and Neptune before heading for deep space. Both Voyagers had a gold plaque mounted that included a diagram showing where the Earth is located in space in case one of them is sometime discovered by intelligent beings far off in the universe. *Voyager 1* encountered Jupiter in March 1979, and *Voyager 2* was slung past Jupiter in July 1979.

THE GALILEO, CRAFT AND MISSION

When the *Challenger* shuttle exploded in January 1986, plans for the Galileo Project had to be changed. Again designed around an umbrella-shaped antenna with RTG power sources extended out on booms, and combining an orbiter and a probe that would descend through Jupiter's clouds, the *Galileo* craft worked from tried-and-true basic designs. The original idea of launching the craft from aboard a shuttle with a rocket that would boost Galileo toward Jupiter had to be scrapped. Instead, an ingenious plan of using several different gravity assists from planets was worked out.

Images gathered from *Viking 2* on Mars continued to reach Earth for five years. *(NASA)*

The *Voyager 2* spacecraft caught this picture of Saturn's rings, showing the alternating dark and dusty rings with the light icy rings of particles in orbit around the planet. *(NASA)*

This was the first space encounter ever with an asteroid, showing a strange, irregular rock pocked with craters, about 12 miles by 8 miles. Later, after looping past Earth, *Galileo* encountered Ida, a potato-shaped object about 35 miles long. Surprisingly, images showed that Ida had its own little moon, about a mile in diameter, orbiting some 100 kilometers or 60 miles out from the asteroid. Although Newton's laws supported the idea that some rocks might go into such little orbits around bigger rocks, this was the first time an asteroid was found to have its own moon. Astronomers later named the little moon Dactyl.

The comet Shoemaker-Levy 9 (SL9) would crash into Jupiter in July 1994, just as *Galileo* was approaching the planet. As the 23 pieces of the broken-up comet smashed into the planet, *Galileo* was about 150 million miles

The new trajectory of *Galileo* would take it past Venus, then in a loop twice past Earth. Changing the plan to send *Galileo* past Venus required better heat protection, as the original design had never been intended for the close approach to the Sun required with a Venus flyby. However, there were some advantages to this spiral trajectory, such as a passage through the asteroid belt with a close-up view of a couple of asteroids never seen clearly before. Furthermore, it was discovered that the comet Shoemaker-Levy 9 would crash into Jupiter while *Galileo* was en route to the planet. *Galileo* would therefore be available to get some good images of the comet crash on that planet. The schedule of the *Galileo* mission is shown in the following table.

Among the astounding pictures sent back by *Galileo* were close-up images of Gaspra-951.

This image of the Moon was captured in 1992 by *Galileo* on its way to Jupiter. *(Courtesy of NASA/JPL/Caltech)*

away from Jupiter, but it retrieved some great photos, relayed back to Earth.

The list of discoveries and new facts uncovered by *Galileo* is extensive. In one report, as *Galileo* flew past Earth, scientists noted that the spacecraft had detected signs of intelligent life on Earth! More seriously, *Galileo* was credited with a long list of discoveries. These

The *Galileo* spacecraft being assembled prior to its 1989 launch *(NASA)*

World's Amateur Explorers and the Shoemaker-Levy 9 Crash

The comet Shoemaker-Levy 9 was discovered on March 25, 1993, by a team of professional and amateur astronomers: Eugene Shoemaker, an astrogeologist; his wife, Carolyn Shoemaker, a planetary astronomer; and David Levy, a writer, editor, and lifelong comet chaser. Soon astronomers began to realize that the comet would strike the planet Jupiter. It became obvious that this was a once-in-a-thousand-years event, demanding a coordinated observation program around the world. As calculations came in, excitement mounted. The collision would occur July 16, 1994. Observatories lined up funding and personnel to be sure to catch the event on film.

By January 1994, the comet had broken up, appearing like a string of pearls stretched out on course to Jupiter. It was no longer a comet, but the plural *comae,* with each piece assuming a tadpolelike shape of a condensed stable core with a long glowing tail stretched behind. As the date neared, astronomers predicted that fragment A would hit the atmosphere of Jupiter at 8 P.M., Greenwich mean time (GMT).

Tom Herbst, a Canadian, headed up a German-Spanish team at the Calar Alto Observatory in southern Spain. On the day of impact, their computer went down a few minutes after 8 P.M. GMT, causing them four minutes of nerve-shattering anxiety. Then, with their telescope and computer back in business, they noticed nothing unusual until 17 minutes after the hour. Suddenly, with cameras taking a steady stream of pictures, they saw the first mark, just at the predicted spot, on the limb, or outer edge, of Jupiter. Shoemaker-Levy plunged into the storms over Jupiter, the greatest collision in space ever filmed.

GALILEO MISSION DATES

Launch	October 18, 1989
Venus flyby	February 10, 1990
Earth flyby (1)	December 8, 1990
Gaspra asteroid	October 29, 1991
Earth flyby (2)	December 8, 1992
Ida asteroid	August 28, 1993
Comet impact	July 1994
Probe to Jupiter	July 13, 1995
Jupiter orbiter data	1995–97

included confirming lightning on Venus, sending back unique images of the polar regions of the Moon, discovering Dactyl, directly observing the SL9 impacts, giving direct data on the impact temperature, and detecting splashback of material from the impacts. Other information included characterizing a large solar flare, observation of the charged-particle magnetosphere surrounding Jupiter as far out as the orbit of its moon Io, collection of detailed chemical and atmosphere information about Jupiter and its moons, and discovery of three previously unknown moons of Jupiter.

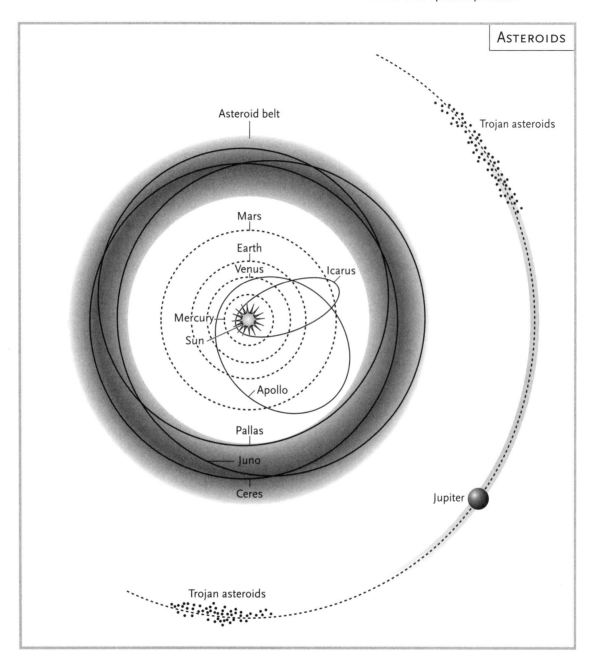

The unmanned explorations by the Viking, Voyager, and *Galileo* spacecraft showed how much could be learned without putting astronauts' lives at risk, and with far less expense. Much of the space exploration of the first part of the 21st century will be through similar but improved unmanned craft.

9

THE *HUBBLE SPACE TELESCOPE*

Astronomers have recognized for centuries that making observations from Earth is unsatisfactory because of the distortion as light travels through Earth's atmosphere. Early space advocates such as Tsiolkovsky, Goddard, and von Braun envisioned a day when rockets would be used to lift telescopic observatories into space orbit, where teams of astronomers and astrophysicists would be able to make startling new discoveries through the clear reaches of space. Although astronauts carried telescopes and cameras on their expeditions out of Earth's atmosphere and to the Moon, the most important observations from outer space have come from unmanned orbiting telescopes. The predictions of the early rocket enthusiasts turned out to be almost right.

In the period from 1991 to 2003, NASA launched into space four "Great Observatories." All of them were unmanned, and unlike most observatories on the mountaintops of Earth, these orbiting observatories were fully automated to respond to instructions sent by radio and to relay the information and images back by radio signal.

The most famous of the four, the *Hubble Space Telescope (HST)*, was an optical telescope, using two mirrors to reflect light from distant stars, galaxies, and the far reaches of space and a charge-coupled device, or detector (CCD), similar to the workings of a digital camera to capture undistorted images. Once the *Hubble*'s equipment was adjusted and operating smoothly, the pictures sent back were truly astounding. Although there were more than two dozen optical telescopes in orbit by 1996 designed to capture light in or near the visual range of the electromagnetic spectrum, *Hubble* obtained the best pictures and provided some of the most exciting new scientific discoveries since Galileo had first aimed his homemade lead telescope at the night sky over Venice.

Less well known to the general public were the three other telescopes, each designed to gather nonvisual radiation from other parts of the electromagnetic spectrum. These included the *Compton Gamma Ray Observatory (CGRO)* launched into orbit in 1991 on a mission that lasted until 2000. The *Advanced X-ray Astrophysics Facility (AXAF),* renamed the *Chandra X-ray Observatory,* was sent into space in 1999 to capture X-ray images of galaxies, planets, the Moon, and other objects in space.

The last of the orbiting telescopes was the *Space InfraRed Telescope Facility (SIRTF),* renamed the *Spitzer Space Telescope* and launched and managed by the JPL in August 2003. The *Spitzer* was designed to operate at near absolute zero temperature, and it took several months to cool down after launch. Scientists around the world proposed research projects and signed up on a schedule to be able to use the infrared observatory once it was in orbit. The images and information gathered by these telescopes have in a few short years vastly increased human knowledge about the age of the universe, its immense size, and the processes by which galaxies, black holes, and stars have been formed and are being formed.

Edwin Hubble

Edwin Powell Hubble was born in Marshfield, Missouri, in 1889. He studied at the University of Chicago and at Oxford University in Britain. In 1914, he joined the Yerkes Observatory in Chicago. In 1919, he moved to Mount Wilson Observatory near Pasadena, California, where he conducted his most important work.

Hubble studied the changes in the spectrum of electromagnetic radiation and light emitted from stars known as the red shift. In 1929, he proposed what became known as Hubble's law, which states that the farther away galaxies recede, the faster they move. He used this principle to define the visually observable portion of the universe. The radius (the distance from the center to the edge) of this sphere of observable space is known as the Hubble radius. Beyond that limit, objects will be moving at the speed of light, so light or other radiation from such sources will never reach Earth and cannot be seen.

Hubble was even better known for his classification of the types of galaxies. Hubble divided all galaxies according to their observable shapes into five main classifications, each subdivided. The five types are elliptical galaxies (ranging from moderately elliptical to fully elliptical), spiral galaxies (classed as Sa, Sb, and Sc, from tightly wound through more loosely wound), barred spiral galaxies with a bar across their centers, lenticular galaxies with no spiral arms, and irregular galaxies.

For a period, astronomers assumed that the classification revealed that galaxies went through an evolution from elliptical to spiral, but that theory has been dropped in favor of the view that one type does not evolve to another. The Milky Way galaxy in which the Earth's Sun is located is assumed to be an Sa or Sb type. From human perspective on the edge of the galaxy, one cannot determine the degree to which the spiral form is tightly wound.

Hubble died in 1953.

HUBBLE:
A Humble Start

The *Hubble Space Telescope* was launched aboard the *Discovery* space shuttle on April 24, 1990, and deployed the next day. The telescope itself just fitted inside the shuttle equipment bay and was the size of a large school bus at 45.2 feet long by about 14 feet in diameter. On launch, it weighed 24,500 pounds. Reaching out like two rectangular wings, large 22-foot-long solar panels provided electricity to operate the equipment that used about 3,000 watts for every 97-minute orbit around the Earth. An American home illuminated by 30 100-watt bulbs might burn as much electricity each hour in the evening. To store the power, *Hubble* carried six nickel-hydrogen batteries that together had the capacity of about 20 automobile batteries.

The optics consisted of two finely ground mirrors. The primary mirror was 94.5 inches in

The *Hubble Space Telescope* in orbit. Owing to a small production error in its main mirror, the telescope produced fuzzy images at first. *(NASA)*

diameter, and a secondary 12-inch-diameter mirror had to be precisely shaped in order to focus the light from distant objects and star clusters. They were designed to lock on a distant star, planet, or galaxy and not deviate more than 7/1000 of an arc second, which represents about the width of a human hair at a distance of one mile. Expressed another way, the lenses could lock and hold on an object that would be the equivalent of a dime held up 200 miles away from the observer.

At a fixed orbit about 380 miles above the surface of the Earth, the telescope moved at just under five miles per second, or about 17,500 miles per hour. Care had to be taken not to focus on or near the Sun, as the light, just as for the human eye, was too powerful for the optics.

As soon as *Hubble* began to observe distant objects, however, astronomers on the ground who looked at the relayed digital pictures were sorely disappointed. While *Hubble* could fix on distant objects, the resultant images did not come through clearly. Instead of a star showing as a point of light, the captured image on the digital record was fuzzy, like a smudge or smear. Corrective computer programs could resolve the images to some extent, but clearly there was something very wrong. After months of investigation, engineers traced the problem to a mistake in the manufacturing process. The finely ground primary mirror, which had to be precise in its shape, was somewhat too flat at the outer edge, a mistake made at the optical grinding stage. The mirror flattened out at its edges by a width of about 1/50 of a human hair. The error caused the focusing defect, or spherical aberration. While the digital cameras worked fine, the light received came in not as a point, but as a halo or fuzzy-edged circle. From the beginning, it had been assumed that a maintenance mission, taking astronauts to do repairs and replacements of

parts would be required, and the *Hubble* had been constructed with special handholds and grappling points so that work could be done on extravehicular activities (EVAs); however, no one had planned to replace the massive and expensive primary mirror.

Engineers decided on a plan to fix a new lens so that *Hubble* would be able to see clearly, just as eyeglasses corrected blurred vision in a human. The first repair mission, scheduled in 1993, was designed to correct the vision problem and also to replace several other parts to extend the life of the telescope. The new parts were packaged as the Corrective Optics Space Telescope Axial Replacement, or COSTAR, and the astronaut crew also took up an improved 620-pound Wide Field Planetary Camera. The new camera had a higher rating and could pick up more light in the ultraviolet range than the original. It also included its own spherical aberration-correction system.

Altogether, four servicing missions were scheduled for December 1993, February 1997, December 1999, and February 2002. The last two had originally been planned as one, but the number of maintenance items included for the third mission expanded so greatly that NASA decided to split that service call into two separate visits.

MISSION STS-61: Fix the *Hubble*

The details of the 1993 repair mission, known as STS-61, received great publicity. Critics of NASA focused on the point that the original telescope had been sent up with a defect in it that should have been caught before the mirror had been accepted. But such criticisms tended to be silenced, once the telescope, with its corrected vision, began sending back spectacular images from the deepest regions of outer space.

Using the space shuttle *Endeavour*, astronauts repair the *Hubble* optics in 1993. *(NASA)*

The space shuttle *Endeavour*, on the shuttle's 59th mission, provided transportation for one of the most important trips ever taken into outer space by delivering the team and the equipment for the repair of the *Hubble*. The team consisted of Commander Richard O. Covey, Pilot Kenneth D. Bowersox, Payload Commander F. Story Musgrave, and Mission Specialists Kathryn Thornton, Claude Nicollier, Jeffrey Hoffman, and Thomas Akers. Their mission to install corrective optics took just four hours short of 11 days and included five EVA sorties. In order to prevent exhaustion from working in the bulky suits and the difficult environment of outer space, the sorties were shared between two alternating shifts of two astronauts each.

On the third day out in orbit, Hoffman spotted the telescope, using a pair of binoculars, and the crew steered *Endeavour* gently closer. Nicollier, a Swiss, used the shuttle arm to snatch *Hubble* and bring it into the bay, where the work proceeded. Although the optics and new gyroscopes were successfully installed and new solar panels were attached, the mission encountered a problem that could potentially mean the end of the multibillion-dollar project: The hatch door to the telescope could not be closed. Specialists on the ground calculated that the problem derived from differential expansion of bolts and other parts due to different temperatures when the hatch was removed. Two astronauts, working together and bracing the hatch between them, were finally able to snap it into place. There were other hitches, too. More than once, astronauts found that their space suits failed initial leak checks, and Thornton's communication system in her suit broke down, requiring that messages be relayed to her by Akers.

After mission STS-61 returned to Earth and the telescope was put through a series of tests, scientists around the world held their breath as they waited for the first new images to come through. What they saw astounded them.

HUBBLE AT WORK

Hubble looked into the center of the galaxy known to backyard astronomers as M87, located in the Virgo cluster. There *Hubble* detected a black hole that had been suspected

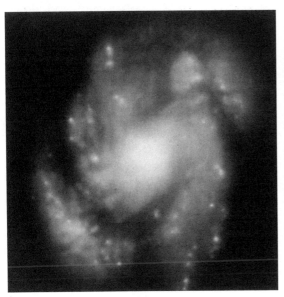 

The galaxy known as M100 was photographed by the *Hubble* before and after the 1993 repair, when the spiral arms of the galaxy became clear. *(NASA)*

but never before detected. In the heart of another galaxy, NGC4261, it found a disc of dust that was 800 light years across, whirling around so fast that the only explanation was that it was held in place by a black hole, calculated to be 1.2 billion times the size of Earth's Sun.

In a different direction, *Hubble* relayed back breathtaking pictures of some 50 stars being born in columns of hydrogen and dust, rising out of a cloud that was itself 6 trillion miles in size. In another shot, *Hubble* found two galaxies colliding and giving off millions of stars. In one small section of the sky near the Big Dipper, never before explored by telescope, *Hubble* found more than 3,000 previously unknown galaxies, each containing millions of stars. The area came to be called the Hubble Deep Field. Looking closer at items in the solar system, *Hubble* detected ozone in the atmosphere of Ganymede, one of the moons of Jupiter, and was able to make out for the first time the ice-covered surface of Pluto. Before *Hubble,* the age of the universe was assumed to be somewhere between 10 and 20 billion years; with *Hubble* recording images of the results of the original big bang, the estimate could be made more accurately: 11 billion years. The CCD system worked so fast that it gathered hundreds of thousands of images on each orbit, creating a vast library of information that scientists would need decades to analyze fully.

CGRO

The *Compton Gamma Ray Observatory (CGRO)* was the second of NASA's four planned Great Observatories. It was named in honor of Arthur Holly Compton (1892–1962), who shared the Nobel Prize in physics in 1927 with Charles Wilson. Compton was honored for his work in the scattering of

high-energy photons by electrons, and he was the first to coin the term *photon* (the quantum unit of electromagnetic radiation, including light). The photon-scattering process was the basis for the gamma-ray detection instruments that were at the core of *CGRO.* Weighing 17 tons, the *Compton* was the heaviest astrophysical instrument ever put into space when

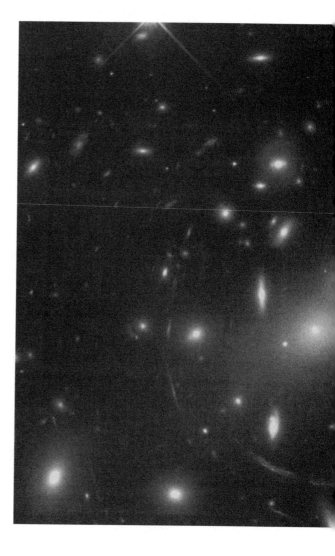

it was launched on April 5, 1991, from aboard the space shuttle *Atlantis*. *CGRO* had four instruments that covered a large part of the gamma-ray section of the electromagnetic spectrum. After more than nine years of gathering data, the *CGRO* was safely "de-orbited" and fell through the atmosphere on June 4, 2000.

CHANDRA

The *Advanced X-ray Astrophysics Facility (AXAF)*, later named the *Chandra Observatory*, contained sophisticated X-ray instrumentation. The Max Planck Institute of Germany contributed crucial parts for the *AXAF*, working with the Space Research Organization of

After the 1999 repair and maintenance mission, the *Hubble* sent back pictures that used the light-bending gravitational field of a galaxy cluster inside the constellation Draco to depict a massive cluster of galaxies beyond. *(NASA, A. Frutcher and the ERO Team)*

the Netherlands, based in Utrecht. The observatory was launched in July 1999, with an expected five to 10-year lifetime. The mirrors aboard the *AXAF* used to focus the X rays were shaped as long tubes, allowing the rays to glance off the interior of the tube and be reflected to a focal point, rather than a more typical parabolic mirror shape, which would create the problem of X-ray penetration into the surface of the mirror.

After a contest to pick a name for the *AXAF*, NASA selected the proposal that it be named for Subrahmanyan Chandrasekhar (1910–95), known to his friends and colleagues as Chandra. In Sanskrit, the word *chandra* means "moon" or "luminous." Trained as a physicist in Madras, India, Chandrasekhar and his wife immigrated to the United States in 1936. He joined the faculty of the University of Chicago. In 1939, he explained the evolution of white dwarf stars in his *Introduction to the Study of Stellar Structure.* He estimated that stars smaller than about one and a half times Earth's own Sun would evolve into white dwarf stars and that stars above the so-called Chandrasekhar limit (now estimated to be 1.2 Suns in size) were likely to explode into supernovae. The remaining mass could either become a white dwarf or a neutron star. In 1983, he shared the Nobel Prize in physics with William Fowler for his theoretical studies of physical processes in connection with the structure and evolution of stars. So *AXAF* became *Chandra*.

NEW TYPES OF EXPLORERS

The *Hubble, Compton,* and *Chandra* were all named after theoretical astrophysicists who had made major contributions in their work to the study of galaxies and stars. Together with ground-based optical and radio telescopes, scientists could now gather information about distant objects in space from a wide range of the electromagnetic spectrum.

Just as the unmanned spacecraft explored the outer solar system, the unmanned telescopes that worked over nearly the whole range of electromagnetic radiation, from infrared through visual light to X rays and gamma rays, allowed ground-based scientists to explore the universe with tools that earlier generations had only dreamed about. As scientists around the world proposed projects and examined the data that poured in from the space-based telescopes, their explorations began to penetrate to the edge of space and time.

10

SEEING TO THE BEGINNING OF TIME

 In 1931, Karl Guthe Jansky, an American researcher at Bell Laboratories in New Jersey, developed a small rotating aerial, which he called the "merry-go-round." His purpose was to detect the sources of the static that kept interfering with early trans-Atlantic broadcasts. The aerial picked up lots of static, which Jansky at first assumed came from thunderstorms or background emissions from engines and other equipment. Jansky noticed that the background hiss of static on his receiver reached an intense level every 24 hours. It moved with the Sun but gained four minutes a day. He realized that this time correlated with the difference in the apparent motion, seen from the Earth, between the Sun and the background stars. He assumed that the source lay outside Earth's solar system, and in 1932, he concluded that it was in the direction of the constellation Sagittarius, toward the center of the Milky Way galaxy. Other radiation apparently came from empty interstellar space. Jansky suggested that Bell Labs undertake the construction of a 100-foot aerial to further investigate these cosmic radio waves, but in the mid-1930s, it was difficult to raise funds for such a venture.

An engineer named Grote Reber built a parabolic-shaped 30-foot antenna in the backyard of his home in Illinois in 1957, and he began to map radio emission from various points in the galaxy. Similar to Jansky, he found the most intense source near Sagittarius. These radio waves had remained a mystery until more sensitive radio equipment, developed during World War II, was applied to the phenomenon. In order to use radio waves to explore space effectively, scientists had to meet a couple of challenges. One was the fact that cosmic radio signals are very faint, representing an extremely tiny amount of energy. In order to gather and magnify the signals, equipment had to be both large and sensitive. Another problem was that to aim and move an antenna of such a large size posed a mechanical difficulty. Such a telescope had to be moved to point in a particular direction in the sky, and then it had to be precisely moved to account for the motion of the Earth in order to remain fixed on the point in space.

Some of the first large radio telescopes designed to sort out and register space radio signals were built in 1948, and some powerful sources were two specific spots in the constellations of Cygnus and Cassiopeia. Two "radio stars," without visible light, were discovered. Soon scientists realized that they could gather a wide variety of information from radio telescopes, including the intensity of the signal, the wavelength and frequency, and the direction of the source.

Over the next four decades, several thousand more radio sources were discovered; for example, the Andromeda nebula, the nearest galaxy to the Milky Way, contains many stars that emit only the 1.80-meter radio wavelength. But these stars produce no visible light. Other sources emit on wavelengths varying over a wide range from a few centimeters up to 20 meters or more. A source in Cygnus was identified as resulting from the collision of two nebulae about 200 million light-years away, meaning that the collision took place 200 million years ago. Radiation at a constant wavelength of 21 meters was discovered in 1951, coming from clouds of hydrogen in interstellar space.

Mysterious, pulsating radio sources, flicking on and off were finally determined to come from rapidly rotating collapsing stars. As one huge star rotated around the other, it would briefly eclipse the radio emission from the first, causing the pulsation in the received signal. Intense sources of radio emission from gas clouds in interstellar space were natural masers, operating on a similar principle to lasers, with radio beams (instead of light beams) focused through the clouds.

PROLIFERATION OF RADIO TELESCOPES

Grote Reber worked from 1954 to 1957 at the Commonwealth Scientific and Industrial Research Organisation in Tasmania, Australia, and from 1957 to 1961, at the National Radio Astronomy Observatory in Green Back, West Virginia. Reber produced a map of radio sources in the universe with wavelengths around 144 meters (473 feet) in length. Bernard Lovell of Manchester University did some of the pioneering work in British radio telescopy. Lovell had worked in the 1930s on radar, and in the postwar years he took over war surplus equipment and set up a team at Jodrell Bank, in Cheshire, Britain, where Manchester University already had an established botany facility. Lovell's first radio telescope, designed to bounce radar beams off the Sun and Venus, was built over the decade 1947–57. In 1957, it was used to track the Soviet Union's satellite *Sputnik 1*. A 250-foot-diameter dish constructed under Lovell's direction remained the largest for some years. Soon the Jodrell Bank receiver was used to assist in mapping the new radio wave–emitting stars, nebulae, and galaxies.

Another British radio telescope receiver system was constructed at Cambridge University, at the Mullard Radio Astronomy Observatory. Rather than using a bowl-shaped receiver, the Mullard system consisted of two cylindrical structures 2,400 feet apart. One was fixed at one spot, and the other moved along a 1,000-foot track.

ARECIBO

Professor William E. Gordon at Cornell University, in New York State, proposed building a large radar antenna that would send and receive signals to study the upper atmosphere, or ionosphere, of Earth. By bouncing radio signals off the thin layers of the ionosphere and reading their reflections, he hoped to learn more about the density and temperature of the region. He calculated that he would need a 1,000-foot-diameter antenna to do the job. However, to construct a movable 1,000-foot-diameter antenna that could be aimed at different points of the sky would be extremely expensive and difficult to engineer. He conceived of the idea of using a fixed antenna bowl, anchored to the ground in one position, with a movable send-ing-and-receiving unit hanging above it. If properly structured, the design would allow the beam to point in a 20-degree range around the point directly overhead. If such a device could be built close to the equator, it would be more useful, as the Sun, Moon, and planets would pass almost directly overhead, well within the 20-degree span of the beam.

Searching for a site, Gordon and his team located a spot just south of the town of Arecibo in the hills of Puerto Rico. Small, deep valleys

The Arecibo radio telescope is set in a natural valley among the mountains of Puerto Rico, surrounded by lush vegetation. *(National Astronomy and Ionosphere Center, Cornell University, National Science Foundation)*

Gregorian Reflector ⟋

The Gregorian reflector system is so-named because it is very similar to an optical system proposed by James Gregory, a professor of mathematics at the University of Edinburgh in 1663. Gregory theorized that two concave mirrors, to focus the light, would eliminate distortion. In his work *Optica Promota*, he suggested a parabolic primary mirror, with a hole for an eyepiece in the center, with an elliptically curved secondary mirror to reflect the light back through the eyepiece hole. Although his idea was very logical, no such telescope could be built at the time, because glass grinders could not produce precise nonspherical curves at the time. Telescopes with two or more parabolic or concave mirrors to catch and focus light have since been known as Gregorian reflector telescopes. The Arecibo radio telescope was improved in 1997 by the addition of a two-reflector system that hangs above the main receiving dish, using the Gregorian principle.

surrounded by steep limestone hills characterize the area's terrain. Some of the valleys had natural sinkholes of limestone that extended deep into the ground. Construction started in 1960 and was finished three years later when the Arecibo Ionospheric Observatory began work. The telescope at Arecibo not only could use the radar beams to explore the ionosphere; by simply using the receiving system, the telescope could also pick up the natural radio emissions of objects in outer space, including Jupiter, the center of the galaxy, and the interstellar masers and double-star pulsars.

Most dish antennas like those used to receive satellite broadcast television are shaped like parabolas. With that type of curve, the incoming parallel beams of energy are focused to a single point where the receiver picks them up. A similar parabolic curve is used in some optical telescopes to focus the reflected light beams to a single point. The Arecibo reflector, however, is not parabolic in shape but rather a section of a sphere. While the parallel energy beams are received and bounced back, they are only partially focused.

This requires that a spherical section antenna have an additional focusing device. One such piece of equipment at Arecibo is a set of line feeds that gather the lower-frequency energy from the spherical section primary reflector. As part of a 1996–97 upgrade, technicians installed a Gregorian feed system that uses second and third radio mirrors to focus the incoming energy. The new system can operate over a wider range of frequencies and is more efficient than the system of line feeds.

Size and Scale of Arecibo

Under the 1,000-foot main reflector dish at Arecibo is an area of about 18 acres, covered with lush undergrowth. The main reflector itself consists of more than 38,000 aluminum panels, supported with a system of steel cables slung across the natural sinkhole in the ground. The aluminum panels, if laid end-to-end, would stretch 227 miles. The Gregorian reflector system itself is suspended 450 feet above the dish and is dome shaped, weighing about 75 tons. It is suspended from a triangular platform that weighs about 700 tons, hung from 18 steel cables. The cables are attached to reinforced concrete towers, that are themselves anchored with cables to the ground. Two of the towers are 265 feet high, and the third, situated on a lower hill, is 365 feet high. The whole structure is so impressive it receives thousands of visitors a year and has even been used as background for an action sequence in the James Bond movie *Golden Eye.*

Even in a high wind, the whole huge hanging assembly moves only a small fraction of an inch, and the cables automatically adjust for changes in temperature so that the angle and height of the platform is accurately maintained. The vast size of the antenna is not only impressive for tourists, it is important to the scientists. It is the largest receiver on Earth, allowing the study of very weak radio-emitting objects in space.

The original cost of the observatory was $9.3 million, with an upgrade in 1974 at a cost of another $9 million. Together with the upgrade completed in 1997 at a cost of $25 million, the facility would now cost well over $100 million to build.

The received electric wavelengths fall in a range from six meters to three centimeters, and with frequencies ranging from 50 megahertz to 10,000 megahertz. With the upgrades in the 1990s, the information is transmitted by cable to computers in the on-site research

The Gregorian reflector hangs over the receiving dish at Arecibo, casting its shadow below. *(National Astronomy and Ionosphere Center, Cornell University, National Science Foundation)*

building, where it can be processed and displayed on video terminals for real-time examination. Some of the data is stored and sent to Cornell University where it is analyzed on supercomputers.

DISPERSED COLLECTION

Robert Hanbury Brown and several colleagues at Manchester University in Britain developed the concept of using several antennas, widely separated, to gain finer resolution of radio sources. At first they disposed of cable linkages, using radio linkages between the receiving antennas and a central computer to record the simultaneously received data. By the 1960s, with the development of very accurate, timed tape recorders, the researchers got rid of any links between the separate receivers and combined the signals from the tapes in a computer. This technique was known as very long baseline interferometry (VLBI). With the development of VLBI, it was then possible to conduct simultaneous observations at widely separated sites around the world. This concept was expanded with the development of the very long baseline array of 10 separate receiving dishes scattered across the United

The 12-meter telescope is located at the Kitt Peak National Observatory, southwest of Tucson, Arizona. Nestled in its protective dome, it did pioneering work in discovering molecules in outer space. *(Image courtesy of NRAO/AUI)*

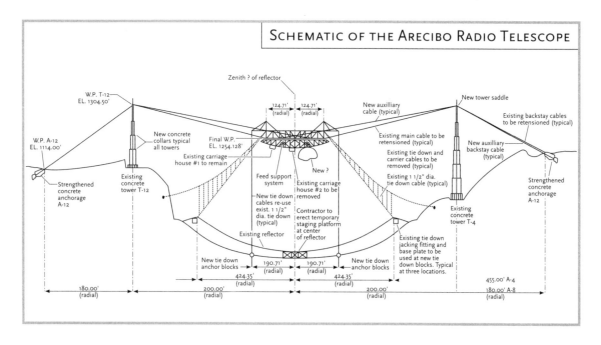

SCHEMATIC OF THE ARECIBO RADIO TELESCOPE

This very large array consists of 27 radio telescopes near Socorro, New Mexico. Computers combine the data from each antenna, making the whole array an interferometer, capable of gathering information from extremely faint distant black holes and galaxies. *(Image courtesy of NRAO/AUI)*

States and several other local arrays elsewhere in the world.

Other radio telescopes, some specializing in very short wavelength emissions have been built. These include a very large array (VLA) of 27 dishes on railcars that can be moved several miles, near Socorro, New Mexico. Other large single dishes include one at Kitt Peak, Arizona, that is 36 feet in diameter, and another more than 125 feet in diameter at Nobeyama, Japan.

BIG BANG OR STEADY STATE?

Just as these improvements in radio telescopes were being developed, astronomers were debating the age of the universe. In 1948, a key paper described what became known as the big bang theory. George Gamow, collaborating with fellow U.S. physicists Ralph Alpher and Robert Herman, argued that the shift of lines in the spectrum of light from distant galaxies that had been documented by Edwin Hubble proved that the galaxies were receding from each other and that the universe was expanding. If the universe was expanding, they argued, at some definable point in the past, the universe must have been compacted. They posited the idea that the universe started at a distant point in time with a "big bang."

British physicist Hermann Bondi, American astrophysicist Thomas Gold, and British astronomer Fred Hoyle opposed the big bang theory. They argued that while the distant galaxies were receding, the universe might be in a steady state, with continual creation of matter. One early problem with the big bang theory was that it appeared that the Earth itself was older than the calculated moment of the big bang, which would be impossible. However, a recalculation of the big bang's age—some 10 to 15 billion years in the past—of the Earth's—at about 4 billion years—reconciled that issue.

Radio telescopes began making contributions to this debate. In 1963, quasars were discovered. These extremely distant objects emitted more energy than anything else did in the universe. They were so far away that their energy had been emitted billions of years ago, suggesting that the early universe was very different from the universe today, a view more compatible with the big bang than with the steady state view.

In 1964–65, American physicists Arno Penzias and Robert Wilson set out to examine the sources of the static that interferes with satellite communication, using a radio telescope and receiver. In this way, their work was similar to the original work of Jansky in 1932, when he discovered the first radio waves from outer space while trying to track the source of radio broadcast static. Penzias and Wilson found a high level of dispersed background radiation at the 7.3 centimeter, or "microwave," wavelength. It was 100 times more powerful than any known source of radiation. When Penzias and Wilson contacted astronomers at Princeton University, in New Jersey, they found that their discovery confirmed predictions of residual microwave radiation from the beginning of the universe in the big bang. Scientists presumed that that background radiation represented a residue of the original big bang. The two Bell Laboratories scientists were awarded the 1978 Nobel Prize in physics for their work.

In these ways, radio telescope discoveries and explorations tended to confirm the big bang. The radio telescope astronomers and the scientists who used the *Hubble Space Telescope* represented a new generation of explorers who traveled through the universe to the very beginning of time.

11

WHAT LIES AHEAD

The exploration of space has been going on since ancient times, as observers studied the night sky above and tried to understand the movements of stars and planets there. But it was only in the 20th century that space exploration got off the surface of Earth. In many ways, the 20th century was the period of human experience where the myths and dreams of the ages began to merge with technology. With the first heavier-than-air flight of Orville and Wilbur Wright in 1903, humans left the surface of the planet to fly in the atmosphere. With the launch of *Sputnik 1* in 1957 and the flight of Yuri Gagarin around the Earth in orbit in 1961, the Soviet Union led the way in taking humans into space. The United States, taking technology as a political challenge, funded massive undertakings to explore outer space with astronauts, first in orbits, then in trips to the Moon, and by the 1980s, with efforts to provide routine travel to outer space aboard shuttles.

The dreamers and the practical engineers brought science fiction and science fact together. As they did so, they encountered deep skepticism and severe criticism. As Marco Polo and Christopher Columbus had centuries earlier, those who sought to travel in space had to fight against scoffers who thought their plans impractical, too expensive, or too likely to fail. The cosmonauts and astronauts became at once the popular heroes of their times and the symbols of a questionable demonstration of human pride and extravagance.

In the Soviet Union, Yuri Gagarin, the first person in space, was immortalized in statues, posters, and postage stamps. He was quiet, modest, enthused, and serious—the perfect model of what a hero should be. On his death in 1968 in an airplane crash, he was mourned by millions of ordinary Russians who loved him as much as members of their family and more than most of the politicians and military leaders who ruled their nation. In the United States, the Apollo astronauts enjoyed a fame that rivaled that of actors, singers, and sports celebrities. In both countries, the governments encouraged the media to make the pilots, technicians, and engineers aboard the craft into larger-than-life representations of the human quest into the unknown.

CONSTELLATIONS FROM THE NORTHERN HEMISPHERE OF EARTH

At the same time, in every country where space travel has been funded from the national treasury, critics have wondered what good would come of the effort. It was fine that scientists learned more about the universe, and it was fine that the United States and the Soviet Union could prove to the world that their technology was advanced. Doubters, however, asked whether the money could be spent more wisely to educate children, cure the sick, provide for the elderly, or any of a hundred other pressing social needs. Even the pursuit of science appeared to be forgotten in the scurry to launch spacecraft and to make some particular spectacular achievement. After all, a fraction of the money spent on the space shuttle or on the Soviet *Mir* station could have funded many observatories on Earth or in orbit and the work of thousands of researchers and scientists in the pursuit of knowledge.

Ice Caps on Mars

Both the north and south poles of Mars are covered by white ice caps that expand and shrink with the seasons. Astronomers speculated whether the ice caps represented reservoirs of frozen water or were frozen carbon dioxide (dry ice).

After the 1976 Viking missions, the debate over dry ice versus water ice was partly solved. At the Martian north pole, the temperatures get cold enough for water to freeze, and water vapor has been spotted over the pole. The temperature is 45 degrees colder at the south pole, allowing the freezing of carbon dioxide. Scientists have assumed that the south pole has both dry ice and water ice. The permanent northern cap is about 1,000 kilometers in diameter, but the southern polar cap is only about 350 kilometers across. Both permanent caps are probably very thin, perhaps just a few meters thick.

In addition to the permanent, or perennial, ice cap, an additional seasonal frost cap grows at both poles. The frosty surface evaporates, with clouds of gas shifting to the opposite pole. When it is summer in the south, the moisture shifts to the north where it is winter, and then shifts back. The seasons are caused, just as they are on Earth, by the fact that the axis of the planet is tipped at an angle to the plane of the planet's orbit, bringing the north and south poles alternately slightly closer to the Sun in half the Martian year.

Mars, like Earth, also goes through long cycles of weather changes. Just as the Earth has suffered ice ages in the ancient past, slight variations in the orbit of Mars probably have affected the climate there, accounting for the disappearance of surface water and changes in the extent of the ice caps over thousands of years.

This photo of Mars from the *Hubble Space Telescope* revealed that weather conditions on the planet include severe dust storms, water ice clouds, and dynamic changes in appearance. *(NASA)*

EXPLORATION OF SPACE FROM EARTH

The exploration of space from the surface of the Earth has been a long tradition. Mathematicians and scientists in ancient Babylon, Mesoamerica, Egypt, Greece, and Rome had developed complex explanations for the nature of the heavens. Although some of their ideas were later proven to be incorrect, many had made observations and calculations that were quite accurate. With the development of the telescope and its use by Galileo in 1608 to study the Moon, the Sun, and the planets, a new era in practical astronomy began. Galileo and many of those who followed him were not experienced astronomers when they began to study the heavens. And as occurred to many of those who came after him, Galileo was regarded in his own time as someone with shocking and irresponsible ideas. He paid the price for his daring in his trial for heresy and house arrest for the rest of his life.

Amateurs and professionals continued to build their own telescopes, improving the designs and constantly learning more over the next three centuries. By the beginning of the 20th century, astronomers had discovered

This artist's conception shows a space interferometry mission spacecraft against the background of a distant nebula. *(Courtesy of NASA/JPL/Caltech)*

An artist's rendering of the Mars Reconnaissance Orbiter which will scan the planet and gather information. *(Courtesy of NASA/JPL/Caltech)*

Robotic spacecraft such as the *Mars Odyssey* gather exploration data at lower cost and with much less risk than manned spaceflight. *(Courtesy of NASA/JPL/Caltech)*

eight of the nine planets of the solar system, had identified all of the major moons in the solar system, and had begun sophisticated study and classification of the galaxies beyond the Milky Way.

Even after the development of Sputnik, exploration of space from the surface of the Earth continued. With improved optical telescopes, with radio telescopes, and with unmanned equipment sent into space, the frontier of knowledge moved back. Some of the greatest 20th-century discoveries about space were made on Earth, using information relayed from space from automated equip-

ment. The most spectacular discoveries came from the *Hubble Space Telescope,* which despite its initial defects, soon produced pictures from light that was emitted at the beginning of time. The advocates of human space travel pointed out, however, that to make the *Hubble* work properly required several teams of men and women to go into space to make essential repairs that could never have been accomplished by remote control.

As astronauts orbited Earth and went to the Moon, many even in the scientific community continued to argue that exploration of space from the surface of the Earth had advantages. In an age in which robotic equipment was being perfected, why risk sending humans to their possible death? Manned exploration, some argued, was not only too expensive, it was unnecessary. An unmanned space probe did not need to carry oxygen, food, water, or garbage and sewage disposal systems. Electrical equipment could work in unpressurized spaces, without air, provided there was an adequate power supply and adequate design to prevent breakdown. All of the observations that a human could make—including the reading of instruments, taking of photographs, and detection of magnetic and radiation fields—could be gathered by robotic instrument and reliably relayed back to Earth for recording, study, and analysis. As long as the rocket carrying such instruments was safely launched and if returned to Earth, safely de-orbited, there was no risk to human life. On the other hand, no robot yet built can achieve on-the-spot decision making, inventiveness, ingenuity, and intuition found in human crews. When robotic devices have broken down in space, more than once, their functions have been lost forever.

THE MARS ROVERS AND FRIENDS

In 2003, NASA launched two robotic explorers to Mars: *Spirit,* on June 10, and *Opportunity,* on July 7. *Spirit* landed January 3, 2004, and *Opportunity* landed January 24, 2004, on different parts of the Red Planet. Part of a longer planned robotic exploration of the planet by several nations, the two rovers had as their first mission detecting the story of past water activity on Mars. With specialized equipment the rovers searched for and tested a wide range of soil and rocks to uncover clues about the history of water on the planet.

Other robotic and unmanned spacecraft, launched by many nations, were scheduled through the first decade of the 21st century, including NASA's Messenger mission to Mercury and New Horizons mission to explore Pluto and its moon, Charon, and continue out to the Kuiper belt of ice pieces in orbit around the Sun far beyond Neptune. Probes launched by Japan and the European Space Agency are scheduled to help explore Mars.

Both the *Spirit* and *Opportunity* rovers landed on airbag-protected systems, then settled onto the surface and rolled out to take panoramic pictures. Over a period of three

One of the projected devices to explore Mars is the FIDO (Field Integrated Design and Operations) rover, tested here in the Nevada desert. *(Courtesy of NASA/JPL/Caltech)*

months, the pictures were analyzed on Earth by scientists to spot promising locations for further investigations. To conduct the tests, the rovers used quite a list of equipment, including the panoramic camera, three different kinds of spectrometers to test the chemical composition of samples and of the atmosphere, magnets to pick up magnetic dust particles, a microscopic imager or camera, and the so-called RAT. The RAT is a rock abrasion tool for scraping the dust and weathered material off samples to allow examination of the fresh material by the onboard instruments. Each rover was equipped with an "arm" to move instruments out to a sample.

The rovers drove from one location to another, up to about 44 yards every day, for a total travel distance of about three-quarters of a mile. By moving from spot to spot, each rover acted like a human geologist, stopping to examine interesting samples, and testing on the spot rocks and soil that seem interesting.

DEBATES ABOUT WORTH

All discovery and exploration has had a dual purpose. On the one hand, exploration leads

A proposed trip of a robotic spacecraft, *New Horizons*, past Pluto and its moon, Charon, is on the agenda of NASA. *(Courtesy of NASA/JPL/Caltech)*

An artist's interpretation of a probe descending to the surface of Saturn's moon Titan. *(Courtesy of NASA/ JPL/Caltech)*

to the increase of knowledge, and increased knowledge is seen by many as a sufficient goal in itself. But the great explorers of the past also opened new worlds to commerce and brought thousands of practical benefits. From the silks and spices of the Orient that were returned to Europe, to the opening of trade with the New World, exploration led to exploitation, and exploitation led to practical profits. While some peoples profited, others often paid a price, being subjugated, enslaved, or forced to work for those who conquered them. Yet the explorers who returned with gold, ivory, spices, furs, silk, and the other riches of the worlds they discovered were able to demonstrate that their trips could turn a profit and produce practical benefits for those who funded the exploration. Exploration and discovery led to contact, conquest, and colonization.

With space exploration by manned or robotic craft, the debate between science and profit continued. In the United States, the Soviet Union, and even in China, there were

One concept for future exploration of other planets involves low-cost, small robotic explorers like these pictured here to gather data on distant planets. *(Courtesy of NASA/JPL/Caltech)*

popular complaints that the expense incurred for gains in scientific knowledge alone was not worth it. By the end of the 20th century with hundreds of satellites in orbit and with the planning for upcoming projects, the space enthusiasts could begin to point to dozens of practical benefits, some already in place, and others looming ahead as possible gains.

Satellites allowed for more accurate weather forecasting, which alone saved millions of dollars. Detailed warnings of approaching hurricanes, for example, allowed coastal dwellers in the United States to board up and prepare their homes and to evacuate well in advance of a storm's arrival. The damage prevented and the lives preserved in one such episode more than paid for the cost of all of the weather satellites ever launched. Furthermore, Earth-scanning satellites provided better knowledge of natural resources on Earth, allowing oil and mineral prospectors to zero in on likely untapped reserves. Remote sensing could provide better analysis of long-range weather patterns and predictions of bountiful or restricted crops around the world, leading to better planning.

For the consumer, benefits from the space age were often quite direct. Everywhere on the planet, people were able to obtain handheld phones that linked by satellite to the world telephone network. With world communication through telephones and television, information was more freely distributed. Even repressive regimes, such as that of the Taliban in Afghanistan or the dictatorships of other nations, could not completely prevent the flow of ideas, information, and entertainment directly into the homes of millions.

Satellites provided detailed military intelligence, allowing the arms control agreements between the United States and Russia to be verified from space, even before the countries agreed to allow on-site inspectors on their

This artist's conception shows the encounter of the spacecraft *Deep Space 1* with the comet Borrelly in September 2003. *(Courtesy of NASA/JPL/Caltech)*

own territories. Military intelligence derived from satellites also allowed the United States and its allies to conduct very successful operations in Bosnia, Kosovo, Iraq, and other trouble spots, with reduced casualty rates and very precise knowledge of the location of enemy installations. Although such information was never perfect, and some tragic errors could and did still happen, satellite information allowed the reduction in the numbers of innocent civilians accidentally killed or injured during attacks on targets of strategic or military value.

The global positioning system (GPS), with miniaturized equipment that could pick up a signal from a satellite to provide a precise readout of the location on Earth of the receiver, allowed for improved navigation and location. GPS was used by scientists and environmentalists to track animal migrations and the melting of glaciers. Emergency crews used GPS to track down medical emergencies, and hikers and explorers used GPS to find their way through remote terrain.

As enthusiasts looked ahead, they came up with other schemes and ideas that might turn a profit from future space exploration. There were plans for mining on the Moon and asteroids. Others considered bringing ice from outer space to increase the planet's water supply. Since space travel itself was such a unique experience (just as airplane flight had seemed in the early 20th century) planners looked forward to arranging tourism in space. While the first flights carrying tourists could charge millions, travel might eventually become so routine that the cost would decline and the numbers increase to make a regular business out of such trips.

THE NEW OCEAN

Despite the expectations of the enthusiasts and dreamers, the debates still remained. Was outer space a new, high frontier for the continuation of the human experience of exploration, or was travel beyond Earth too inherently risky? Should space only be explored from Earth, using robots, radar, telescopes, and remote equipment to gain knowledge more cheaply and more safely?

By the early 21st century, dreamers still advocated manned trips to Mars. Detailed plans for "terraforming" Mars had been developed: Engineers and environmental scientists were researching ways to plant crops on Mars that would help bind the windblown soil and increase the oxygen in the atmosphere, eventually bringing the Red Planet up to a quality that would sustain human life. Science fiction author Ray Bradbury's pictures of colonies on Mars seemed much more possible and closer to realization. Serious planners evaluated the detailed costs and arrangements involved in launching colonies of thousands of travelers aboard large vessels to voyage through space for hundreds of years and for many generations to eventually arrive at distant solar systems.

The debates continue. On January 14, 2004, President George W. Bush proposed an ambitious plan for human exploration on the Moon and Mars. Those with the dreams and the plans argue that technology makes such visions much closer to reality. Others suggest that the fortunes that would have to be spent and the risks that would have to be incurred make such concepts grossly impractical. Science, they say, could gain far more, much more cheaply and at much less risk to life, by remote robotic probes and by Earth-based gathering of data.

The lure of the high frontier, the new ocean of space remain. Tomorrow's citizens will continue to debate how it is to be explored.

Glossary

aberration   A deviation from planned performance of a device; in optical telescopes, the distortion of an image due to built-in characteristics of the lenses and mirrors.

asteroids   Pieces of rock and ice, most of which orbit in the region between the orbits of Mars and Jupiter. Other groups of asteroids, known as the Trojan asteroids, precede or trail Jupiter in its own orbit. Asteroids range in size from several hundred miles in diameter to the size of houses and smaller.

astrologer   A practitioner of the art of predicting human behavior based on the motions of the planets and other distant objects. *Astrology* is the method of making such predictions; generally regarded by modern astronomers as without foundation in fact.

astronautics   The term was coined in the 1930s to refer to the engineering and science fields connected with developing craft capable of traveling into outer space, patterned after the term *aeronautics,* which described airplane design and engineering. In the United States, those traveling aboard spacecraft have been called *astronauts.*

astronomer   Either a professional or amateur scientist who observes objects in outer space and studies their motions, makeup, and relationships. *Astronomy* is the name of this study.

astronomical unit (A.U.)   The distance from the Sun to Earth is regarded as one astronomical unit. It is about 93 million miles or about 8.3 light-minutes, meaning that it takes about eight minutes for light to travel from the Sun to Earth.

astrophysicist   A scientist who studies the physical makeup of stars, galaxies, and other distant objects, which is known as *astrophysics.*

big bang theory   Astronomical observations have led scientists to conclude that the universe began approximately 11 billion years ago with a single explosion that sent matter and energy speeding apart. As observations of distant galaxies are gathered with advanced equipment, increasing evidence is gathered to give credence to this theory and to provide details as to the nature of the universe in its first seconds of existence.

black holes   Observation from advanced telescopes that gather either visual light or other radiation have led astronomers to conclude that there are objects in the universe that are so dense that their gravity attracts all nearby objects and light to fall into them. Although not truly "holes" in the universe, but rather extremely dense objects, their effect is like that of a hole in that whole stars fall into them and disappear.

canali In 1877, the Italian astronomer Giovanni Schiaparelli described markings that he observed on Mars as *canali,* which could be translated as "channels." However, since the word *canal* implies intelligent construction, other observers leapt to the conclusion that the presence of the *canali* demonstrated that there was intelligent life on Mars.

Canopus star tracker A device aboard unmanned spacecraft to identify and lock on the direction and angle of the star Canopus. When an onboard computer compares the angle to that of the Sun, the orientation of the spacecraft can be established.

celestial Pertaining to the heavens. Ancient astronomers believed everything on Earth obeyed terrestrial, or Earth-bound, laws, while the heavens contained celestial objects that were by nature pure. Observations of the Moon by telescope revealed that the Moon, like Earth, had mountains, suggesting similarities between celestial and terrestrial conditions. Today the term simply refers to all space and objects in it beyond the Earth's outer atmosphere.

charge-coupled device (charge-coupled detector, CCD) This electronic part is the key element in digital cameras, allowing the registry of spots of light and the conversion of them into numerical data that can be stored or transmitted electronically. CCDs allowed the transmission by radio of clear images from satellites and space exploration vehicles.

comet Numerous comets, consisting of ice, dust, and gases, rotate in elongated orbits around the Sun. Some comets return periodically and have been carefully studied, while others are discovered every year. When they enter the inner solar system,

they are heated by the solar wind and by radiation, emitting particles and gases in illuminated tails that can often be observed from Earth, sometimes without the aid of telescopes.

command module On the Apollo missions to the Moon, the command module orbited around the Moon, while the lunar module descended to the surface and then lifted off to rejoin the orbiting command module.

constellation A grouping of stars as viewed from Earth. Since from the perspective of Earth, near and far stars may appear clustered together, a constellation may include stars that are not in a true group or cluster.

corporate culture The habit, customs, rules, and ways of doing business that characterize an organization. The corporate culture of NASA was the subject of criticism after the loss of space shuttles.

cosmic rays Streams of atomic particles present in outer space, apparently emitted by distant stars and galaxies. When these atomic particles collide with the outer atmosphere of Earth, they generate subatomic particles, most of which are classed as mesons, that shower the Earth.

cosmodromes The launching stations for space rockets in the Soviet Union and now in present-day Kazakhstan and Russia.

cosmonaut A space traveler, or astronaut, in the Soviet, now Russian space programs. It derives from *cosmos,* another term for outer space.

crystalline spheres In ancient times, astronomers concluded that the planets and stars had to be held up in the night sky by some invisible substance. Claudius Ptolemy and others concluded that spheres made of a crystal substance, revolving one inside the other, could account for the fact that stars do not fall from the sky and also for their independent motions.

de-orbiting Bringing down a satellite or spacecraft from space to Earth. When a satellite has outlived its usefulness, it is sometimes brought down from orbit to crash on Earth in a safe zone such as an empty area of an ocean. Such a procedure is safer than allowing the orbit to gradually decay, as that could lead to a crash in a populated area.

drogue parachute A small parachute used to pull another large one out from its container or package.

ecliptic plane The plane of the orbit of Earth around the Sun. Most of the planets of the solar system rotate around the Sun in roughly the same plane as Earth (within two or three degrees of Earth's plane of orbit), as if they were circles drawn on or in a thin pancake around the Sun at the center. However, the orbit of Pluto is "eccentric" in that it is tipped about 17 degrees to that of Earth's orbit.

electrical and environmental command officer (EECOM) The person in ground control of space missions who is in charge of electrical and environmental issues.

electromagnetic spectrum Oscillating electric and magnetic fields travel through space at about 186,000 miles per second. The wavelength ranges on a spectrum, progressively shorter from long radio waves through shortwave radio, microwaves, and radar to infrared light, visual light, ultraviolet light, X rays, and gamma rays.

expendable rocket Rockets that can be used only once to launch satellites or other spacecraft. Expendable rockets either crash in an ocean or desolate area, or burn up on reentry into the atmosphere.

flight dynamics officer (FIDO) The person in ground control of space missions in charge of the craft's flight path.

flyby Passing without stopping or orbiting. Numerous spacecraft have conducted a flyby of a planet, asteroid, or moon in order to gather data.

galaxy A vast cluster of stars. Galaxies are classified by their shape, either in the form of spirals, barred spirals, or less defined shapes. Millions of galaxies have been observed with telescopes, such as the *Hubble Space Telescope*, which orbits around the Earth.

geocentric Earth-centered. Claudius Ptolemy (ca. 100–170 A.D.) developed a model of the universe in which the Sun, Moon, and planets revolved around the Earth. This Earth-centered solar system model is known as a geocentric model.

gravity assisted trajectory A pathway through outer space that is enhanced by a relatively close passage near a planet or moon to pick up speed from the planet's gravitational field. Several manned and unmanned space exploration missions have made use of this "slingshot" effect to reduce the need for fuel and to extend the reach of the spacecraft.

Gregorian reflector A secondary, small mirror used in astronomical devices, including both optical telescopes and radio telescopes, to bring the received waves into focus back through a hole in the primary reflecting mirror. It is named after James Gregory, a 17th-century Scottish professor who suggested the design.

ground control The engineering and management staff based on Earth that stays in communication with astronauts on manned missions, providing analysis of information and instructions based on that information.

heat shield A conical or dish-shaped piece of heat-resistant material, usually a ceramic, used to protect a space vehicle on its return to Earth through the atmosphere. The friction of rapid descent raises temperatures above the melting point of metals.

heliocentric   Sun-centered. Nicolaus Copernicus (1473–1543) theorized that the motions of the planets in the solar system as they appear from Earth could be better explained by a model of the solar system with the Sun at its center, rather than the Earth, as presumed under a geocentric model.

Hubble constant   The rate at which the universe is expanding, about 45 miles per second for every million parsecs of distance from the Earth.

Inquisition   In response to divisions in the Catholic Church and to the growth of disbelief in Christianity, the Roman Catholic Church created the Inquisition in the 13th century. The Inquisition served as courts that would inquire into charges of heresy against individuals. In Spain, Italy, France, and elsewhere, those found guilty would be punished by the civil authorities, with punishments ranging from house arrest or warnings to imprisonment, torture, or execution.

instrumentation and communications officer (INCO)   The person in ground control of space missions in charge of communication.

intercontinental ballistic missile (ICBM) During the late 1950s, the Soviet Union and the United States began to construct rockets capable of delivering a nuclear weapon to a target in the other nation's territory. Under arms control agreements negotiated in the 1980s and 1990s, many ICBMs have been eliminated.

interferometry   A technique used in radio astronomy in which signals from different radio telescopes are combined by computer to construct a high-resolution image of a distant object such as a star or galaxy.

ionosphere   The outer layers of the Earth's atmosphere, from about 38 miles to 620 miles up, containing gases that are ionized, that is, whose atoms are broken down by radiation into positive and negatively charged particles.

kilometer (km)   The equivalent of .621 miles.

light-year   The distance traveled by light or other electromagnetic radiation at the speed of about 186,000 miles per second over the period of a year. Expressed another way, a light-year is equal to about 10 trillion kilometers.

lunar module (LM) or lunar excursion module (LEM)   The part of the Apollo spacecraft that descended to the surface of the Moon, then later rejoined the orbiting command module.

magnetometer   In space exploration, a device for measuring the strength or intensity of the magnetic field of a planet or a moon.

magnetosphere   The volume of space around a planet that is controlled by the planet's magnetic field, acting as a magnetic shell. The shell deflects the solar wind around the planet.

mares   The dark, relatively smooth areas of the Moon, once thought to be seas, or *mares* in Latin. Closer telescopic observation and human visits to the Moon have determined that the mares consist of dust and gravel.

mile   The statutory mile used in the United States is 5,280 feet, equivalent to about 1.609 kilometers.

module   A major section or part of a spacecraft. Space stations are often designed with numerous connected modules with different functions, such as laboratory, workshop, living quarters, and service facilities.

navigation The science of finding one's location in reference to other known locations. Navigation at sea improved over the centuries with the development of the compass, the sextant for detecting the elevation of the Sun and stars above the horizon, the accurate chronometer or clock, and accurate charts and maps. Navigation is accomplished in near outer space by sightings of the Earth's horizon, and in more distant space, by locating a particular known star and computing the angle between that star and the Sun.

neutron star A small and very dense star, consisting mostly of neutrons. Some neutron stars are thought to contain the mass of as many as 20 of Earth's Suns, compressed into a sphere no more than 12 miles in diameter.

Nobel Prize The inventor of dynamite, Alfred Nobel, left his fortune to support the awarding of prizes in different fields of science. Beginning in 1901, annual prizes are awarded in the fields of chemistry, physiology or medicine, and physics (as well as literature and peace). Often, two or more scientists share the prize, which includes a medal and a very large cash award.

orbit The pathway of one object around another in space. The orbit of Earth around the Sun is not precisely circular but rather a slightly elongated ellipse, with a mean distance to the Sun of about 93 million miles, or 149.6 million kilometers.

orbiter Any spacecraft that goes into orbit around a planet. More specifically, the space shuttles are classed as Orbiters. Built by NASA between 1981 and 1993 six craft were designated as "orbiter vehicles," although only five were designed to go to orbit. Two of the fleet have been lost in accidents.

O-ring A rubber gasket in the shape of a circle that is used to separate two parts of a machine. In the Saturn rockets used as the first stage to lift shuttles into space, the fuel tanks are separated by large O-rings that were discovered to be unsafe in extremely cold weather.

parabola A specific type of curve, formed mathematically by cutting a cone by a plane held parallel to one side of the cone.

parsec Measure of distance equal to about 3.2616 light-years.

probe In space exploration, an automated vehicle or craft that descends through the atmosphere of a planet. Probes to Jupiter are destroyed in the atmosphere of the planet, while probes to some other planets have successfully descended to the surface of the planet to conduct tests.

quasar A contraction of *quasi-stellar*, a quasar is a starlike object found outside galaxies but that emits radiation on the scale of 100 large galaxies.

radioisotope thermoelectric generator (radio thermal generator, RTG) A device for generating electricity from the differential heating of two adjacent metals warmed by the decay of a radioactive isotope. RTGs were used in several early unmanned spacecraft as power sources.

radio telescope A device for receiving electromagnetic radiation from distant stars or other objects that is emitted in the radio wave part of the spectrum. Radio telescopes have been built on Earth and have been placed in orbit.

redshift The lengthening of wavelengths from objects in space produced by the rapid movement of the objects away from Earth. The color of the object shifts down the electromagnetic scale, in the red direction, hence the name. By measuring the redshift, the speed of an object can be estimated.

retrofire officer (RETRO) The person in ground control of space missions in charge of the timing of retrofiring rockets to slow the spacecraft.

retrograde motion The apparent shift in the position of a planet in the night sky of Earth, from a regular forward motion to an apparent loop back in its own pathway. The apparent retrograde motion is due to the changing locations of both the Earth and the observed planet.

satellite, artificial and natural A satellite is an object revolving around a larger one. The Moon is a natural satellite of Earth. Since 1957, humans have launched by rocket hundreds of artificial satellites to revolve around the Earth.

shuttle In space exploration, any one of five spacecraft designed to be lifted into orbit by heavy rockets and to return to Earth in a controlled glide. Five operating shuttles have been constructed—*Challenger, Columbia, Discovery, Atlantis,* and *Endeavour*—in addition to the *Enterprise,* which was built to test some characteristics of the craft but not designed for orbit.

solar system The group of planets and other objects, including Earth, that revolve around the Sun. There are nine planets as well as numerous moons, comets, and asteroids in the solar system.

solar wind The stream of atomic particles flowing out from the Sun at speeds between 200 and 600 miles per second. The particles are mostly electrons and protons. Some of the solar wind comes in gusts or bursts, causing interference with cell phone and radio receivers. Traveling slower than light, a burst of solar wind from an observed flare on the Sun may take a day or more to reach the Earth's magnetosphere.

space station An orbiting facility in space, constructed by taking separate modules into space and connecting them in place, and designed to accommodate a crew aboard to conduct experiments and do other work. The Soviet, later Russian, space station *Mir* operated for about 15 years. The *International Space Station* was partially constructed by 2004.

spectrometer A device used to analyze the radiation emitted by a distant object. The spectral information collected can be used to determine the chemical composition of the distant object and also to measure the redshift of light and so determine the speed of the object away from Earth.

stage A step in rocket firing sequences. In space travel, rockets are often stacked so that those with the heaviest lifting capacity fire first, carrying smaller rockets aloft for separation and later ignition. The initial firing of the heavy-lifting rockets is the first stage, with later ignitions numbered thereafter.

subsystem In engineering, a subsystem is an interrelated set of parts that perform a specific function within a larger system. Thus, for example, in a spacecraft, the atmospheric supply system for astronaut breathing will include subsystems for the removal of carbon dioxide and contaminants.

telemetry officer (TELMU) The person in ground control of space missions in charge of monitoring information on a craft's performance and status.

trajectory The pathway of a projectile or missile, often in the shape of a large arc that can be described as a parabolic curve.

zodiac The ancient astronomers of Babylon identified 12 constellations across the sky through which the Sun would rise at different times of the year, and through which the planets would cross on their paths through the heavens. Each of the constellations covers about 30 degrees of the night sky, and all 12 of them lie along the horizon when viewed from parts of the Northern Hemisphere of Earth. They are Aries, Taurus, Gemini, Cancer, Leo, Virgo, Libra, Scorpio, Sagittarius, Capricorn, Aquarius, and Pisces.

FURTHER INFORMATION

NONFICTION

Aldrin, Buzz, and Malcolm McConnell. *Men from Earth.* 2d ed. New York: Bantam Books, 1991.

Armstrong, Neil, Michael Collins, and Edwin E. Aldrin, Jr. *First on the Moon.* Boston: Little, Brown, 1970.

Baker, David. *The History of Manned Space Flight.* New York: Crown Publishers, 1981.

Belton, M. J. S., et al. "Galileo's First Images of Jupiter and the Galilean Satellites." *Science* (October 18, 1996), pp. 377–385.

Benson, Michael. *Beyond: Visions of the Interplanetary Probes.* New York: Harry N. Abrams, 2003.

———. "Celestial Sightseeing." *Smithsonian Magazine* (November 2003), pp. 64–72.

Brooks, Courtney G., James Grimwood, and Loyd Swenson, Jr. *Chariots for Apollo: A History of Manned Lunar Spacecraft.* Washington, D.C.: National Aeronautics and Space Administration, 1979.

Bulkeley, Rip. *The Sputniks Crisis and Early United States Space Policy.* Bloomington: Indiana University Press, 1991.

Burke, B. F., and F. Graham-Smith. *An Introduction to Radio Astronomy.* New York: Cambridge University Press, 1997.

Burrows, William E. *Deep Black: Space Espionage and National Security.* New York: Random House, 1986.

———. *Exploring Space.* New York: Random House, 1991.

———. *This New Ocean: The Story of the First Space Age.* New York: Random House, 1998.

Carpenter, M. Scott, et al. *We Seven.* New York: Simon and Schuster, 1962.

Chaikin, Andrew. *A Man on the Moon: The Voyages of the Apollo Astronauts.* New York: Viking, 1994.

Clarke, Arthur C. *The Exploration of Space.* New York: Harper Brothers, 1951.

———. *The Making of a Moon.* New York: Harper Brothers, 1957.

Collins, Michael. *Carrying the Fire: An Astronaut's Journeys.* New York: Farrar, Straus, and Giroux, 1974.

———. *Mission to Mars.* New York: Grove Weidenfeld, 1990.

Columbia Accident Investigation Board. *Report.* Washington, D.C.: National Aeronautics and Space Administration, 2003.

Committee on Human Exploration, Space Studies Board, National Research Council. *Scientific Prerequisites for the Human Exploration of Space.* Washington, D.C.: National Academy Press, 1992.

Davis, Joel. *Flyby: The Interplanetary Odyssey of Voyager 2.* New York: Atheneum, 1987.

Diamond, Edwin. *The Rise and Fall of the Space Age.* New York: Doubleday, 1964.

Fogg, Martyn J. "Terraforming Mars: Conceptual Solutions to the Problems of Plant Growth in Low Concentrations of Oxygen." *Journal of the British Interplanetary Society* 48 (October 1995): 427–434.

Goldsmith, D. *The Astronomers*. New York: St. Martin's Press, 1991.

Greenstein, G. *Frozen Star: Pulsars, Black Holes, and the Fate of Stars*. New York: New American Library, 1983.

Hacker, Barton, and James Grimwood. *On the Shoulders of Titans: A History of Project Gemini*. Washington, D.C.: National Aeronautics and Space Administration, 1977.

Hawthorne, Douglas B. *Men and Women of Space*. San Diego, Calif.: Univelt, 1992.

Heppenheimer, T. A. *Countdown, a History of Spaceflight*. New York: Wiley, 1997.

———. *Development of the Space Shuttle, 1972–1981*. Washington, D.C.: Smithsonian Institution Press, 2002.

———. *The Space Shuttle Decision: NASA's Search for a Reusable Space Vehicle*. Washington, D.C.: Smithsonian Institution Press, 2002.

Jenkins, Dennis. *Space Shuttle: The History of the National Space Transportation System—The First 100 Missions*. North Branch, Minn.: Specialty Press, 2001.

Kennan, Erlend A., and Edmund H. Harvey, Jr. *Mission to the Moon: A Critical Examination of NASA and the Space Program*. New York: William Morrow, 1969.

Kowitt, Mark E., and Michael S. Kaplan. "The Wings of Daedalus: The Convergence of Myth and Technology in 20th Century Culture." *Journal of the British Interplanetary Society* 46 (November 1993): 439–443.

Laeser, Richard P., William I. McLaughlin, and Donna M. Wolff. "Engineering Voyager 2's Encounter with Uranus." *Scientific American* (November 1986): 36–45.

Launius, Roger D., and Dennis R. Jenkins, eds. *To Reach the High Frontier: A History of U.S. Launch Vehicles*. Lexington: University Press of Kentucky, 2002.

Lehman, Milton. *Robert H. Goddard*. New York: Da Capo Press, 1963.

Ley, Willy. *Rockets, Missiles, and Space Travel*. New York: Viking Press, 1968.

Lovell, Bernard. *The Story of Jodrell Bank*. Oxford, U.K.: Oxford University Press, 1968.

Lovell, Jim, and Jeffrey Kluger. *Apollo 13*. New York: Simon and Schuster, 1995.

McCurdy, Howard E. *Inside NASA*. Baltimore, Md.: Johns Hopkins University Press, 1993.

McDougall, Walter A. *. . . the Heavens and the Earth: A Political History of the Space Age*. New York: Basic Books, 1985.

McKay, David S., et al. "Search for Past Life on Mars: Possible Relic Biogenic Activity in Martian Meteorite ALH84001." *Science* (August 16, 1996), pp. 1,639–1,643.

McSween, Harry Y., Jr. *Stardust to Planets: A Geological Tour of the Solar System*. New York: St. Martin's, 1993.

Murray, Charles, and Catherine Bly Cox. *Apollo: The Race to the Moon*. New York: Simon and Schuster, 1989.

National Astronomy and Ionosphere Center. *Arecibo Observatory*. Ithaca, N.Y.: Cornell University, 1997.

Needell, Allan A., ed. *The First Twenty Five Years in Space*. Washington, D.C.: Smithsonian Institution Press, 1983.

Oberg, James E. *Red Star in Orbit*. New York: Random House, 1981.

Ordway, Frederick I., III, ed. *History of Rocketry and Astronautics*. Washington, D.C.: American Astronautical Society, 1989.

Ordway, Frederick I., III, and Randy Liebermann, eds. *Blueprint for Space: Science Fiction to Science Fact*. Washington, D.C.: Smithsonian Institution Press, 1992.

Ordway, Frederick I., III, and Mitchell R. Sharpe. *The Rocket Team*. New York: Thomas Y. Crowell, 1979.

Peterson, Ivars. *Chaos in the Solar System*. New York: W. H. Freeman, 1993.

Presidential Commission on the Space Shuttle Challenger Accident (Rogers Commission). *Report*. Washington, D.C.: Government Printing Office, 1986.

Sagan, Carl. *Cosmos*. New York: Random House, 1980.

———. *Pale Blue Dot.* New York: Random House, 1994.

Smoluchowski, Roman. *The Solar System.* New York: Scientific American Books, 1983.

Spencer, John R., and Jacqueline Mitton, eds. *The Great Comet Crash: The Collision of Comet Shoemaker-Levy 9 and Jupiter.* New York: Cambridge University Press, 1995.

Tsiolkovsky, Konstantin. *Beyond the Planet Earth.* New York: Pergamon Press, 1960.

von Braun, Wernher. *The Mars Project.* Urbana: University of Illinois Press, 1991.

Weaver, H. A., et al. "Hubble Space Telescope Observations of Comet P/Shoemaker-Levy 9 (1993)." *Science* (February 11, 1994), pp. 787–791.

Wilford, John Noble. *Mars Beckons: The Mysteries, the Challenges, the Expectations of our Next Great Adventure in Space.* New York: Knopf, 1990.

Winter, Frank H. *Prelude to the Space Age—The Rocket Societies: 1924–1940.* Washington, D.C.: National Air and Space Museum, 1983.

Wolfe, Tom. *The Right Stuff.* New York: Farrar, Straus, and Giroux, 1979.

Yenne, Bill, ed. *Interplanetary Spacecraft.* New York: Exeter Books, 1988.

Zubrin, Robert, and Richard Wagner. *The Case for Mars: The Plan to Settle the Red Planet.* New York: Free Press, 1996.

FICTION

Bradbury, Ray. *The Martian Chronicles.* New York: Bantam, 1979.

Clarke, Arthur C. *2001: A Space Odyssey.* New York: New American Library, 1982.

Heinlein, Robert A. *The Puppet Masters.* Garden City, N.Y.: Doubleday, 1951.

———. *Red Planet: A Colonial Boy on Mars.* New York: Scribner's Sons, 1949.

Verne, Jules. *From the Earth to the Moon, and Round the Moon.* New York: Dodd Mead, 1962.

Wells, H. G. *The First Men in the Moon.* Jefferson, N.C.: McFarland, 1998.

———. *War of the Worlds.* Jefferson, N.C.: McFarland, 2001.

VHS AND DVD

Apollo 13. Dir. by Ron Howard. MCA Universal, 1995. VHS and DVD.

Mars—The Red Planet Collection: Life on Mars; Destination Mars. Discovery Channel, Brentwood Home Video, 1996. VHS and DVD.

NASA—25 Years: The Greatest Show in Space; The Eagle Has Landed; Houston, We've Got a Problem—Apollo 13 the Real Story; Apollo 15 in the Mountains of the Moon; Apollo 16 Nothing So Hidden. Madacy Entertainment Group, 1995. VHS box set.

NASA—25 Years: Opening New Frontiers; We Deliver; Launch and Retrieval of Satellites; Satellite Repairs. Madacy Entertainment Group, 1997. VHS box set.

NASA—50 Years of Space Exploration: The Story of America's Courageous Space Explorers. Madacy Entertainment Group, 1999. DVD collection.

2001: A Space Odyssey. Dir. by Stanley Kubrick. MGM, 1968. VHS and DVD.

Star Wars Trilogy: Star Wars; The Empire Strikes Back; Return of the Jedi. Prod. by George Lucas. 20th Century Fox Home Video, 2000. VHS and DVD.

WEB SITES

CGRO Science Support Center. Available online. URL: http://cossc.gsfc.nasa.gov. Downloaded on November 7, 2003.

Chandra X-Ray Observatory Press Room. Available online. URL: http://chandra.harvard.edu/press. Downloaded on November 7, 2003.

HubbleSite Reference Desk. Available online. URL: http://hubblesite.org/reference_desk. Downloaded on November 7, 2003.

International Space Station. Available online. URL:http://www.shuttlepresskit.com/ISS_OVR/index.htm. Downloaded on November 7, 2003.

NASA Mars Exploration Rover Mission. Available online. URL: http://marsrovers.jpl.nasa.gov. Updated on January 29, 2004.

NASA Planetary Photojournal. Available online. URL: http://photojournal.jpl.nasa.gov. Downloaded on November 7, 2003.

NASA SpaceLink: Human Exploration and Development of Space. Available online. URL: http://xsl.msfc.nasa.gov/NASA.Projects/Human.Exploration.and.Development.of.Space/index.html. Downloaded on January 15, 2004.

NASA Space Shuttle Launches. Available online. URL: http://science.ksc.nasa.gov/shuttle/missions/missions.html. Downloaded on November 7, 2003.

Solarviews.com. Views of the Solar System. Available online. URL: http://www:solarviews.com. Downloaded on November 7, 2003.

INDEX

Page numbers in *italics* indicate a photograph. Page numbers followed by *m* indicate maps or diagrams. Page numbers followed by *g* indicate glossary entries. Page numbers in **boldface** indicate box features.